Memories from my Past

The Story of a Ten Pound Pom Girl

By
J. B. Duncan

Copyright © 2024 by J B Duncan & Christine K. Duncan
All Rights Reserved. No part of this publication may be reproduced, distributed, or transmitted in any form or by any means, including photocopy, recording, or other electronic or mechanical methods, without the prior written permission of the author. For permission requests or enquiries, please email the author at christinekyrin@gmail.com

First published 2024 Sweetfields Publishing House
Wingham 2429
N.S.W. Australia

ISBN: 978-0-6458910-6-5

Edited by Moonlit Magic Creations.
Cover design (front) Joyce B. Duncan
Cover art and back cover design and art, Interior Graphics/Art Credit: Christine K. Duncan
All pictures (except personal family photos), including pages 12, 17, 75, 90, 93 & 103 and all historic advertisements and newspaper images, are classified Public Domain, sourced from Internet copyright-free sites. All remaining images not included in Picture Credits at rear of book supplied by Christine K. Duncan or Clive.

Because of the dynamic nature of the Internet, any web addresses or links contained in this book may have changed since publication and may no longer be valid. The views expressed in this work are solely those of the author and do not necessarily reflect the views of the publisher, and the publisher hereby disclaims any responsibility for them.

The author of this book does not dispense medical advice or prescribe the use of any technique as a form of treatment for physical, emotional, or medical problems without the advice of a physician, either directly or indirectly. The intent of the author is only to offer information of a general nature to help you in your quest for emotional and spiritual wellbeing.

In the event you use any of the information in this book for yourself, the author and the publisher assume no responsibility for your actions.

This book contains the names of people of actual events. In many instances permission to reproduce their names has been granted by the person, or persons, involved (including those who have since died pre, or during, the writing process of this book). In some instances, said person(s) have chosen to be given an alias. Other names cannot have been requested for permission due to the deceased nature of the individual. As these were related to the author, it is the author's choice to use real names. The surviving relations of said peoples remain free of endorsement of this book. For those names for which permission has not been gained, and where names may be used, the application of an alias may also appear.

Acknowledgements

I would like to thank my husband for his patience while I was writing this remarkable life's story, I have enjoyed sharing it with you. I hope my beautiful daughter has not suffered too much while writing this book, although I know she put everything in her own life aside to get it this far!

Her many hours helping me with recalling my memories, the many more hours in typing them up, fixing any errors and making it all flow together, plus the countless days and late nights (often into the early dawn) she spent hunting around and accumulating photos, cards, old magazine and newspaper ads or labels, checking and rechecking their dates and details, and putting everything in place from front cover to back cover – I cannot thank her enough!

Her skills with the computer have amazed me, and I love the wonderful cover and bookmark she has made too. Without her help, I could not have done any of it myself! I also thank my dear friend and publisher, Maureen Larter, for her patience over the last few years waiting for this book to be finished.

I also would like to thank my beautiful spirit guides who inspired me to write it. They have stayed with me throughout my entire journey, prompting me when I was not sure how to express my thoughts. For this I am grateful, I love you all, thank you for being in my life.

Regards,
Joyce

This is a heart-warming story of a young girl's journey from childhood traumas to adult traumas, and her wonderful holidays to wonderful friends, too.

I loved this story and feel I have travelled this journey with her.

H. M. Hollywood
Counsellor A. M.

A heart-warming story of a lady's journey of enlightenment and spiritual growth. A truly gifted medium and gentle soul.

Thank you for sharing your story Joyce.

Rev. Jason Nicholson JP CMC
International Council of Spiritualist
Manning/Great Lakes Spiritualist Centre

Dedicated to…
My husband Clive, and daughter Christine.

Also to my Dad, my Mum,
brother David, and sisters Hilda and Brenda,
Grandma Hollywood, Aunty Maude,
And my beautiful son Arthur –
Now all in spirit
I love you very much!

CONTENTS

Introduction   1

PART ONE: The Early Years

Sunderland	4
Dad's Greenhouse	12
School	16
The New Baby	21
Grandad Hollywood	23
The Nottingham Farm	26
Penshaw Monument	28
The Walk to Seaburn Beach	29
The Day I Nearly Drowned	32
Dad Leaves for Australia	35
Moving Overseas	42
The S. S. Cameronia	46

PART TWO: Australia

Australian Waters	58
Castor Oil	61
The Long Ride West	66
Warragamba	68
Australian Schooling	71
The Awful Alsatian	74
Running Away	76
The Black Doll	81
Otford	86
A Lot of Bull	93

CONTENTS

PART TWO: Australia (contd.)

A Pain in the Bum	95
The Half House	98
Being Cinderella	102
Clive	108
Out of Control Mother	112
Dundas	118
Changing Jobs	124
Recovery	134
The Griffith Holiday	140
My Twenty-first Birthday	147

PART THREE: A New Family

Getting Married	152
The Sleep-out	164
Finding A Name	170
Our First Home	179
My Son's Health	187
Another Baby	196
Dad, I Love You	206
A Peek-A-Boo Baby	214
The Crash That Killed Me	233
Postscript	242
The Boarding House	243
Picture Credits	246

Introduction

Early one morning, three weeks before I began writing this book, I had a spirit lady come to me. I was waking up with the sun when I heard a lot of voices talking, and this particular lady's voice said to me, "You have to write another book."

It sounded like Lydia, the spirit lady who came to me in 2012 and inspired me to write my first book, *My Encounters with the Spirit World*. I must have drifted back off to sleep, for next thing I remember, she was saying something more.

"You must tell people what happened to you leading up to this first book."

"Why?" I asked her.

"Everyone who has read your books have been helped in some way, whether they've been comforted, or relieved to know they are not alone in their grief, or have learnt that they do have spiritual gifts and they are to honour them by developing them further and growing spiritually. And they want to know what happened to you leading up to your abilities to see and hear spirits."

"Well," I began cautiously, "if this is so, where do I start, and what will I say?"

"You just pick up your pen and paper and I will help you."

Then just like a counsellor, she fired the questions at me, prompting me to find my answers. This is how it started.

This is not a spiritual book; it's about my journey from childhood to now, and the experiences that shaped my life. My first question was…

"When and where were you born?" she asked. "And in what? Remember? It was the war and the Blitz was on."

I remembered, and I'm sure my poor mother remembered that only too well through her life!

Then this lady took me through my age groups, asking me various things, making me remember my memories from the past of so long ago. I am over eighty now! We went right up until I reached my tenth birthday, when at this stage, my family moved from England to Warragamba Dam, in Australia.

Then with my daughter's help, we went over things again, and I began to remember more and more. I continued talking about significant experiences of my life from my childhood, through my teens, up to my adult years. Moving out of England to Australia was a big thing, while growing up in this new country was hard.

I was intrigued by all of the things I could remember, and it helped me to understand my life, and my Mum, a *lot* more than ever before.

So I begin my journey here with you. I will start at the beginning with my first question from Lydia.

෴

Memories From My Past

The Early Years

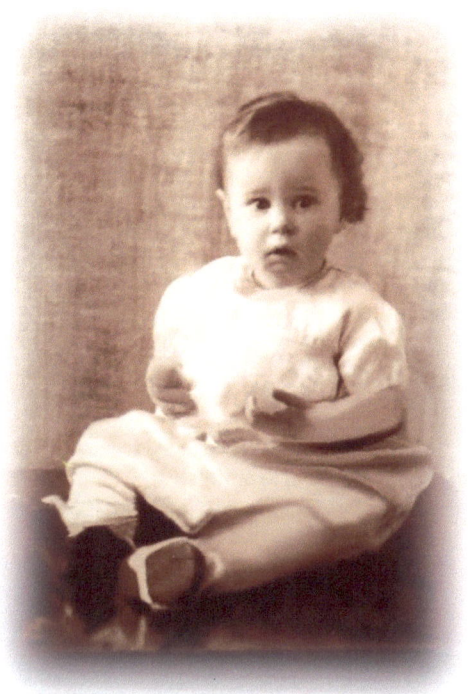

Sunderland

My life began with a bang – or should I say, a bomb. I was born in the last week of August, 1940 in Sunderland, England, in an air-raid shelter while bombs were being dropped. It was the Blitz, and the shelter was just a short walk up a small hill from Mum and Dad's house.

As soon as the warning siren went off, everyone knew they had to run for their nearest shelter and to stay there until it was safe to return home. I can imagine my poor mum, heavily pregnant and ready to drop, hearing the sound of possible doom and having to grab my older twin brother and sister and race up that hill as fast as they could.

It was around mid-afternoon when she heard the siren going, and it was the following morning when I was born. Mum often said that I must have been wondering what was going on, and that I had wanted to see it for myself. She said that I wouldn't wait, so she tried sitting on me to stop me from coming out, but that hadn't worked for her. I expect she would have been terrified of giving birth as a bomb fell overhead, and she must have struggled to hold me back for as long as possible, no doubt preferring to give birth *after* the attack, and in better surroundings.

An example of an air-raid shelter.

But I had wanted out so badly, she'd said, and so there I was, a newborn in a crowded, concrete bunker. My brother, David, and sister, Hilda, were apparently cared for by some friends in the shelter at the time.

My father, poor thing, was a volunteer fireman, so he was off with his brigade during this attack, tending to fires caused by the bombs, or looking after people in need of help. Fortunately our street was spared a direct hit, but a lot of other homes in our town weren't.

Firemen at work in a bomb-damaged street in London, after a Saturday night air raid, ca. 1941.

When I was older, I remember him telling me of a very sad story where, in one building he'd gone into, he saw the mutilated bodies of a man and woman lying in their bed, and a bomb had gone down right through the middle between them, killing them instantly. It had affected him greatly, leaving him often depressed.

I've since read that Sunderland was one of the towns that had suffered the worst bombing by the Germans, with more than 270 people having died from them between 1940 to 1941!

At long last, a few days after I was born, the call came through: it was safe to return to our homes. Though they would have been shaken, Mum and us kids went back to our house, no doubt relieved to find it still intact.

***

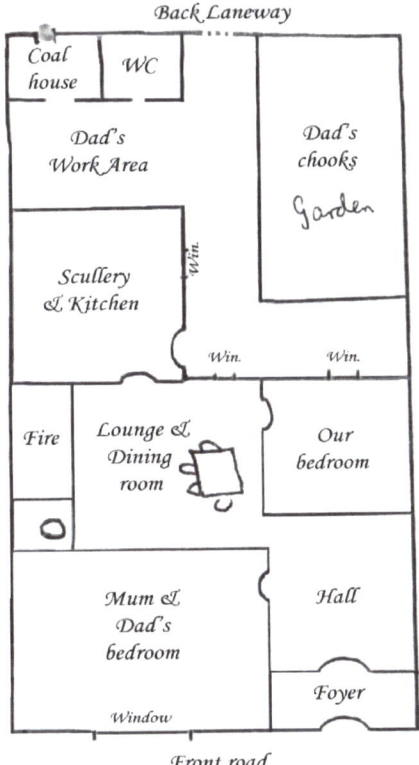

Above: A modern photo of our house in Sunderland. Dad loved to put displays in this front window at Christmas.

Right: My sketch floor plan of our house in Sunderland (not to scale).

    Our home in Sunderland was very small. From the foyer, as you walked into the hallway, there was a room to the immediate left; that was Mum and Dad's bedroom. The hallway then dog-legged into a combined dining and lounge room area, where a raised wood fireplace stood against the far wall. It had an iron grill over it that Mum put to good use. From boiling the kettle for hot drinks and filling the bath, to roasting meat in a big heavy frypan and cooking the vegetables in a cauldron, it seemed to always be going, especially in the cold winter. To the left side of the fireplace was a heavy, oblong iron box that she baked our bread in.

    Off this dining area was a bedroom that we kids shared, with a double bed to fit all three of us! Being the tiny one, I slept between David and Hilda. We had a tiny kitchen, called a scullery, at the back of the house, where Mum prepared the vegetables, and a toilet, (called a water closet, or WC) way down at the back of our yard next to the coal shed, with Dad's work area between them.

Everything about this place was small, but that's all Mum and Dad could afford.

A photo of our backyard, looking towards the back wall and gate (David & Hilda as infants, & Rover the dog, beside the chook pen).

***

Mum had to go back to work as soon as she could, so as a toddler, I was left with relatives who lived close enough and who could help her out. David and Hilda were going to kindergarten when I was only three, and I quickly came to love my Aunty Maude, Mum's eldest sister, mostly as she spoiled me.

But 1944 is a year I don't wish to remember, as there was one uncle I really hated. I had just turned four, and Mum's brother, Tom, had offered to look after me.

I can't express the horror and pain I experienced at the hands of this uncle, and though I try to, I can't forget those awful weeks with him – and then, also with his mate – alone in our house. There is no way to describe the filth and degradation a child feels with an adult predator, especially when it is one you are supposed to trust. I won't go into detail, I can't because it is too painful. Just to say that what he did to me, and what he made me put up with between him and his mate, has affected me all my life.

Carnal child abuse gives victims a sentence of guilt and fear, and all sorts of mental punishment that we carry in our heads for years, often to our graves. It is one of the very worst crimes people commit. He would say to me to not tell Mum, "because it's our little secret", and if I did, he would deny it, and I would then get a belting from her because I'd lied. Silly me believed him!

News 1944: Glenn Miller goes missing.

I feared my Mum, too, because in those days, there were no laws against smacking kids and adults commonly beat them red raw. I honestly thought that she would believe her brother over me, and I'd get an awful beating from her. So I never said anything to anyone, not even right up until after I was married. I've hated him ever since and I really hope he got what he deserved when he died many years later!

***

I was glad when the school holidays came, because Mum was able to stay home and be with me. Two weeks before Christmas, her older sister – my Aunty Maude, (whom I loved) – came for a visit, bringing Uncle Tom with her.

On this day I was playing on my Hobby Horse, which had a metal framework and a wooden body covered in light stuffing and furry fabric. It had

metal wheels on its feet and a metal handle, so I could push it around like a pram. But this horse also had a stiff, short tail, which would prove to be dangerous.

While scooting around on it, I fell backwards and the tail slid up the inside of my legs, cutting me in between my groin.

I screamed with pain and Mum picked me up, while my beautiful Aunty grabbed some towels. They rushed me to my room, where a towel was thrown on the bed. Mum lay me down and began pressing the other towels on the cut to stop the bleeding. We didn't have telephones at home to ring for a doctor or an ambulance, and it was too far to get me to the hospital. So with no phone, or car, Mum had to do whatever she could to help me. She told me to rest until the bleeding stopped, and I was packed up with cloth nappies.

But the whole time my ugly uncle was eagerly staring at me over her left shoulder, watching every move she made with me! His smile was dirty and frightening.

I wanted to scream at him to go away, but I thought that if I did, Mum would want to know why. So I kept quiet, frozen with fear. His filthy smile still haunts me to this day.

***

Anyway, my next happy moment was when I turned five. I started school – yee-ha no more carers!

News 1945: Adolf Hitler dies.

I enjoyed my early years there. I was taught how to "play shops", how to pay for things and how to give change to customers. I also made lots of friends. One girl in particular, Joan

Fishwick, became my best friend, and we stayed friends until I was ten, when my family moved. I lost contact with her because I didn't know how to send letters to people.

***

Left: A shopkeeper cancels the coupons in a British housewife's ration book for the tea, sugar, cooking fats and bacon she is allowed for one week. Most foods in Britain are rationed and some brand names are given the designation "National".

Just after the war, like everyone else, Mum was issued with a ration book of tickets to buy food. In those days you didn't get paid a lot of money, and in that time of war, these ration books helped the poorer people buy their food. Everything was in short supply and probably expensive, that the poorer people got these ration tickets to help towards their food shopping, while their pay went on bills, but there were limitations to what you could buy.

You didn't just go in and buy a packet of tea or sugar in those days, or a bottle of milk. You went up to the Grocer and told him what you wanted, such as half a pound of sugar.

He'd then get a brown paper bag and go to a big hessian bag, where the sugar was kept, and measure out the requested quantity, pouring it into the paper bag with a scoop.

Right: An example of a child's ration book. Throughout the 1940s (and for nine years after the end of the war) everyone in Britain owned ration books of coupons for food and clothing.

A ration book might only give the holder the value of say, five pounds; I remember Mum had a five-pound note one time and I think that was probably Dad's wage for the week! For this, Mum got a ration of two pounds with her tickets, and that had to last us a week, so we had to get essential items only. As I recall, the ration tickets could only be used on certain days for certain items.

Getting the shopping for Mum was a chore Hilda and I had to do. We would go to the general store (opposite the park where we would play) with Mum's big cane-woven basket, and hand over the right number of tickets for the groceries she wanted. Then on different days, there were other shops down the road and around the corner, where we could get bread and soft drinks, like Sarsaparilla.

༄༅

News 1945: America drops two atomic bombs on Japan (Aug.)

Dad's Greenhouse

I also remember Dad's greenhouse. English ones were typically rented out on a separate piece of land, called an allotment, as houses often didn't have much of a yard. If you watch any English murder mystery, you'll see them everywhere, allotments with greenhouses on them.

So, because you couldn't have a proper garden with your house, you would rent out this bit of land and put your own thing on it – and lo and behold if someone went in your rented yard and started eating your fruit or vegies! I'd say that somebody must have been looking after them, because you would get into trouble if you were found in somebody else's allotment, especially if you had no real excuse for being there.

An example of an English greenhouse on an allotment.

Some people had small blocks and others had bigger blocks, and they could use it for growing plants or maybe for use as a chicken pen. Quite a few allotments had greenhouses, and some grew all kinds of vegetables in them. Dad had built his own one (about the size of a single deck bus) and he had a lock on its door. It was roughly about half an hour's walk from home, and I can still remember that we would go to the bottom of our street, turn left, and just follow the road until we reached the greenhouse.

He grew some lovely tomatoes and carrots, and

some other green-leaf vegetable that might have been cabbage or cauliflower, I really don't recall what it was. But I liked to help pick the tomatoes so I could eat one on the way home!

I think it was just me and Dad, because Hilda and David were out always off doing their own thing, and Brenda was a baby and Mum was always just coddling her. I think that was why Dad and I were always so close. I was almost like the son he never had. I *think* I should have been a boy, because I would have been Dad's right-hand boy. And I used to help Dad wherever I could.

***

We would often call in to see my dad's parents as we passed their street (though it was more often Grandma Duncan we saw). It wasn't far from the allotment, possibly about ten minutes' walk, but they were very pleased to see us each time. Dad would always offer them some fresh vegetables, which they appreciated. Grandma was always pleased to see us, and if Grandpa Duncan was there, he was typically rolling his tobacco in front of the fire, not saying very much.

Dad in his 20's or 30's near his allotment, on his way to his parent's house.

But this year was a bad one for Dad, as both of them died within six months of each other. I was only about five, and never saw much of Grandad Duncan, really. It was only those visits and the few times he might have been asked to look after me when I saw him – and even then, all he did was roll his tobacco while I played with my toys. About all I knew of him was that he used to smoke a tobacco pipe.

I don't know what caused either of their deaths. In those days, kids weren't told what they died of. But from what I'm later led to believe, he went in his sleep, although it was probably cancer that had really got him in the end.

Grandma Duncan went a few months after him, because, it was said, she was lonely, she was on her own.

"We've got to go up to Grandma Duncan's house," Mum said to me one particular day, "because she's not very well."

When we got up to the house, we were allowed to go in, but only as far as the hallway. I remember standing there, looking into the dining room at this long wooden box on the table. When people died in those days, they were laid out in the coffin on the table, often in the front room, or parlour. I didn't know this back then, and Mum didn't tell me she'd actually died. This was the first time I'd seen a coffin. I didn't know what they were used for.

"All kids stay out there please!" someone said to us, and so we had to wait for the adults to stand around this big, long box, talking away and looking inside it. I was waiting to go see Grandma lying sick in bed.

After a little while they all went into the kitchen, which was the room right next door. I was curious about what was inside the box and, getting a bit bored, I wanted to have a look in there too.

'Well, no one's watching,' I thought, and snuck into the room.

I climbed up onto a chair and caught a glimpse of Grandma's face. She looked just like she was sleeping.

'Why don't you wake up, Grandma?' my little mind wondered. *'We're all here to see you?'*

But suddenly I was seen.

"Hey you!" one of the older aunties shouted, pointing her hand angrily. "Out! Out!"

I instantly climbed back down, afraid I was going to get a smack.

"Go on! Get Out!" she insisted. "Out of there!"

I ran as fast as I could to Mum, hoping she'd hide me and not be cranky too.

༄༅

School

Early February of that year also meant I went into First Grade at school. My old school, (that's no longer there) was one big long building made up of lots of rooms inside: each room was a class of kids all of the same grade. We would sit at lots of desks that ran the length of the room, with an inkwell in the middle of each for us all to share. My Kindergarten class, for example, probably had about thirty kids in it, with two kids at each table.

The grounds out the front of this building was divided in two halves by a railed wooden fence with a gate in the middle. Kindergarten and Infants classes played in the left side yard, and the older kids played on the other side – and you got in big trouble if you went through the gate and were caught out on the wrong side!

I was so thrilled when the teacher asked me if I wanted to be made the class Milk Monitor! In those days, schools gave the kids a small bottle of milk every morning at around ten o'clock. They came in a crate that the government provided, and two older boys were elected to carry it in to the hallway and leave it just outside of our classroom door. Then I had to give out the bottles, with a straw, to each of the kids. We sat at our desks to drink it, then, when we were finished, I would collect the empty bottles and put them back in the crate. Then we were allowed to go outside to play. I felt honoured that I was chosen for the job!

At lunch time, (the English term was 'dinnertime'), when the bell went, we had to go into this big hall just outside our classroom to eat. Very long tables were set up in rows, and food was given for those

In the spring through to summer, when the weather was warmer and the sun was shining, I would often walk up to the same hill we had slid down in the winter.

There were three or four bench seats up there and I would enjoy lying on one and just gazing up at the clouds, trying to see if I could make pictures out of them. I remember seeing rabbits, dogs, even faces sometimes. I would lay there for over an hour, with no interference from anyone. I loved watching the clouds drift by! When I got tired of this, I would simply get up and walk back home.

***

Dad was a larrikin, or a bit of a joker. Here he is (on left), mucking around dressed as a woman, leaning on a mate. He loved to entertain and make people laugh. He was such a good-natured man and was well liked. He's probably about mid-late 20's in this photo.

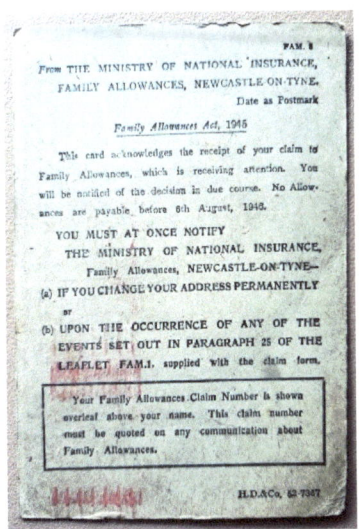

Above & right: Mum's Family Allowance card from the Government.

One day Mum surprised us. In the August of 1946, when I had turned six, she announced that she was going to have a baby just after Christmas. We couldn't wait. Was it going to be a boy or a girl?

I also remember that just before Christmas arrived, we ran out of coal for our fire.

"Take Joyce down to the coal yard and get some coal in the pram," Mum said to David and Hilda one day.

I think Mum had gone into the shed only a few weeks earlier to fish out this cane pram that she had used for us when we were babies. She'd cleaned it up and was probably expecting to use it for the new baby due in two months. She must have thought it a good idea to collect the coal with it, because now it was going to be used as our wheel barrow.

A pram like what Mum had.

We didn't mind helping Mum because she was expecting what would be our little sister very soon. So David and Hilda took me along to the coal yard, pushing the empty pram down the road ahead of them. Even though the distance to the yard was only about ten minutes' drive by car, it took us kids around twenty-five minutes to walk. Naturally, I got tired.

Being older than me, they walked faster, too, and soon I was running behind them, crying, "I'm tired! I'm tired! Can I hop in the pram?"

They slowed up and let me climb in. It was so much fun, being able to watch the world go by without having to puff and pant behind them! I even lay down and dozed!

When we arrived at the coal yard, I had to get out, of course, as there was no room for me – and it would have been very uncomfortable too. It also meant there would be no comfy ride back home, either! So we got the pram loaded up with coal and turned about, with David and Hilda pushing, and little me dragging up the rear! It took us forty-five minutes with the extra weight, but I made it home, *very* tired.

***

Sunderland streets under deep snow January-February 1947

For over two weeks we were covered in heavy snow. The sun didn't come out even once in that time. Tram cables were brought down and roads were blocked, and the electricity to our homes was cut off, making life even harder. It was so cold!

Christmas came and then January moved into February. There were lots of times when we got snowed in. It would come up to around two or three feet, (or sixty to ninety cm) at our front door. In the winter of 1947 it was really bad. I remember going to the front door and opening it, seeing the snow piled up higher than me! Mum told us kids to go get the shovels and move the snow, as we couldn't even get out to go to school until a path was cleared! So we got the shovels and started moving it to one side. It would be up past my waist at times! Sometimes when the snow got too deep, a truck with a sort of bulldozer-front would go round the roads, clearing it for the cars to be able to drive.

I remember getting out my sled and going up to the end of our street where the air raid shelter once stood. It was gone now and I think it got filled in, because a little hill had formed there, to around the height of a single-deck bus. Us kids would walk up this hill and jump onto our sleds and slide down to the roadway. It was great fun!

There would be around fifty or more people up there and no one got harassed by anyone. We kids all felt safe. But we couldn't do that sort of thing today. It's sad to say, but I feel that little kids of today would likely be molested or even kidnapped! Yet there we were, allowed to play up to ten o'clock at night sometimes before having to go home to bed, (in the north of England, the sky doesn't turn dark until about then, unlike in Australia, where it goes from daylight to night very quickly, as I was to find out later!). Those days were both fun and safe, and I remember them fondly.

The New Baby

It was 1947 and I was now six-and-a-half years old when Mum was ready to have the new baby. I remember the night our little sister was born very well.

David, Hilda and I had been sent to bed around nine o'clock, though we were wondering how long we had to wait for the birth. Eventually we fell asleep, and it was well after midnight when Dad came into our room and woke us up. Excitedly he babbled that the baby was about to be born and did we want to see it. We all jumped up and out of bed and ran down the hall and stood outside of Mum and Dad's room.

In those days, fathers weren't allowed in with the mothers when babies were born, so he had to wait outside with us, too. It seemed like hours had passed, but it was possibly only one hour later when we heard a sound I had never heard before. I looked to Dad, very confused. I thought Mum had had a cat in there too.

"Is that a cat screaming?" I asked him.

He gave a gentle laugh. "No," he said, "that's the baby! Mums had it at last!"

After a little while the midwife came out.

"Would you like to see your baby sister?" she asked.

"Yes!" we all said.

She took us in to see her. By now she had stopped crying and she was cradled in Mum's arms. She looked so tiny.

"Say hello to your new little sister," Mum said.

"Oh gee she's tiny! What's her name, Mum?" I asked.

"Well, I think we're going to call her Brenda," she said.

You could see how proud Dad was with her, and probably very relieved that it was finally all over. I don't think we went back to bed for ages that night!

೧೦೦೩

News 1947: Famous reporting of a U.F.O. having crashed in Roswell, U.S.A.

Grandad Hollywood

I remember from a very early age – I think I must have been around four or five – when we used to walk to grandma's house and sit around the fireplace with her, telling her silly jokes. This was my Mum's mother, Grandma Hollywood, and I loved her.

But after a few months of turning seven, maybe around Christmas time of that year, we heard the bad news that Mum's Dad, (Granddad John Hollywood), had died.

I don't recall much about him, because I rarely saw him anyway, and whenever we went to visit them, he'd disappear from the house. To me, it was like men didn't like their grandkids and didn't want to have anything to do with them. Grandma (Anne) Hollywood was always left to look after us. So his death didn't affect me that much; I don't even remember going to his funeral.

I think, though, that the news came as a bit of a shock to everyone else, and poor Grandma was heartbroken. From what I can understand of things, he was a harsh man; not what you could say was brutal, but he certainly wasn't a very kind father. I suppose it may have had something to do with having gone to war.

Grandma and her husband were very close, and in the months that followed, we visited her once or twice a week, or as often as we could, to try and cheer her up. I don't know if we succeeded, but it was always nice to see her. I remember going in with David and Hilda, and all we did was tell her funny, stupid jokes, like…

We'd say, "Why did the chicken cross the road?"

"Ooh I don't know, you'll have to tell me," she'd say.

We'd try and come up with some funny answers, or we'd just laugh aloud anyway without giving an answer. I'm sure she must have heard it so many times already, yet she laughed along with us like it was a new joke.

Sometimes you could see she was upset, but she never seemed to let on to us just how bad it was for her.

I cherish those times I'd had with her, and still do.

***

My Mum was sad, but that was about all, it seemed. She went off to work every day and nothing happened, but you could see she was affected. I think she got on better with her Mum, whereas her and her Dad might not have been that close. I mean, she'd had three other sisters and a brother to share him with.

I do recall that she'd cried for days, though. Most of the time I could hear her sobbing, but didn't actually see it. She may have been in her room, or at the kitchen sink, and she'd sniffle. But she didn't want to show it in front of us. Sometimes she was hanging out the washing, and I would see her wiping a tear from her eyes. I could feel her hurting, but as a kid, I didn't really understand why.

Because I hadn't been close to him, it didn't sink in what kind of a loss it was for the adults. It's only after my own Dad died that I realised why Mum was crying so much. She obviously loved her father!

For the first three to four months after his passing, Grandma Hollywood regularly saw a bright light, like an orb, around her.

Whenever Mum visited her, she would excitedly tell her that, "Your father came to me again last night!"

Apparently every night when she went to bed, this torch-like light came into her bedroom from one corner, swooped right over the top of her, and then went out to the other side of the room. She was delighted to see it, too. She believed it was her husband, and accepted this as being his way of saying hello to her, and that he was okay. Many, many years later I learned that these two had first met on a railway platform and liked each other from the start!

ಬಂಗ

Nottingham Farm

Also while I was around seven, Mum and Dad took us to Nottingham in the summer holidays, (July to August), where my father's relatives had a farm. We had to go by bus, which was about four or five hours south of Sunderland. Dad couldn't drive us, and I think that's because he couldn't afford to buy a car!

A bus like the one we went on to the farm in Nottingham.

We had never been to a farm before and us kids had a ball of a time there feeding the cows and goats, and of course, the chooks. I even got to feed some baby goats and lambs!

Watching my uncle work so hard was also great. I didn't know there was so much work to do on a farm! Uncle 'John' used a pitch fork on these huge hay bales; he'd load them onto the wagon behind the tractor and let us kids climb up to ride on top of them to the paddocks. The cows came from everywhere when they saw what was happening. Then Uncle spread the bales apart as he tossed it from the wagon, and they came running eagerly.

He had grain pellets for the sheep, and we enjoyed watching him round up the sheep with their pet dog and herd them to the troughs where their food had been poured. We learnt about where milk and eggs

came from on that trip – I actually saw him milk a cow once, using the bucket method, and we helped collect the eggs, which could sometimes still be warm if they'd been freshly laid.

When it wasn't work time, we were allowed to play in the yard and the hay shed, and climbing over the bales was so much fun. David, Hilda and I loved playing Hide-and-Seek there, too, as there was lots of new and exciting places to hide in.

My aunty gave us breakfast in the summer house, just off the side of the main house itself. It was a small trellis room covered with smelling vines. It was heavenly! She introduced me to a cereal I hadn't heard of, called puffed wheat. I thoroughly enjoyed it and had them every morning.

But then, sadly it was time for us to go back home. I didn't want to leave, but unfortunately we had to. On the last day, I even asked if I could stay with them, but Mum said no, I had to go back to school.

I think if I had been given the choice, I would've gladly stayed with them, but sadly, I couldn't.

Dad beside a tractor at the farm.

𝒫𝑒𝑛𝑠𝒽𝒶𝓌 𝑀𝑜𝓃𝓊𝓂𝑒𝓃𝓉

Wood Carving at Barnes Park.

I also remember the picnics we went on during some of our school holidays. Mum would pack a big lunch and Dad got the blanket and we'd catch the bus to a local park about half an hour away. I think it was called Barnes Park, but I am not quite sure, all I know is that when we arrived, we would walk through the big gates and up a slight pathway to a beautiful spot near the mulberry bushes. Dad would spread out the blanket and Mum took the food out of the basket and we'd wait eagerly for the sandwiches. After eating, we could play and Mum would let us pick the mulberries. Most got eaten but some managed to make it home for cooking.

Every Easter, she would cook boiled eggs for us to paint, because the next day after Sunday school, we would get on the bus and go up to a beautiful place called Penshaw Monument, that sits on top of a very steep hill. It looked like a Greek temple with columns all around the sides, and it's still there today, where you can see for miles.

When we reached the top, we would have fun rolling down this hill, then run back up and roly-poly down again. After a while, we would then roll our eggs down the hill, rolling down after them and if they cracked, we would peel off the shell and eat them. It was great! After a couple of hours, we would then pack up and head for the bus, and boy we were tired when we arrived home!

Left: Penshaw Monument.

⊱⊰

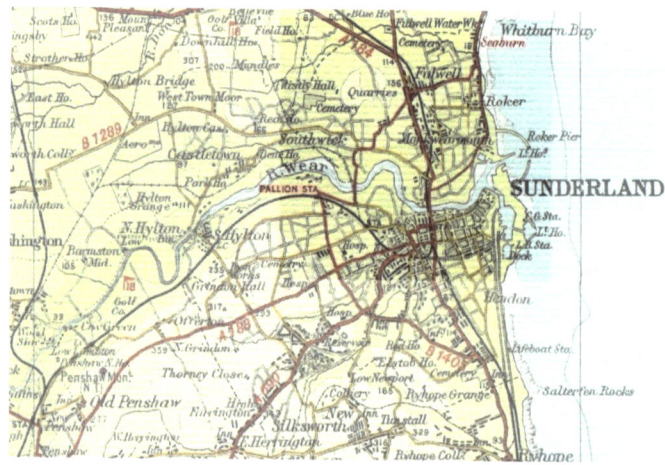

The Walk to Seaburn Beach

In the summer just before I turned eight we had a very hot day.

in early summer when I was getting ready for school, and Mum told me of her plan for the day.

"Dad and I are thinking of going to the beach today, so when you get home, if we are not here, just get changed into your swimmers, then put a dress over you, then come down to the beach. I will leave the bus money for you on the table."

"Okay," I said, and went off to school.

When I came home, they had gone to the beach as planned. As it was only a short distance away, I did what Mum told me. I put on my swimmers and then a dress over the top, but I couldn't find any money left out for the bus ride. I didn't have any money of my own; I was eight, and we didn't get pocket money either – Mum couldn't afford it. So I decided to walk there.

I didn't know if there was a short cut, so I followed the bus route, not realising how far the beach was going this way, and on foot. Luckily it was safe to walk long distances in those days and it took me around an hour before reaching the sand, but I enjoyed the stroll. When I found Mum and Dad, she was anxious.

"What happened?" she asked. "What took you so long? Did you miss the bus?"

"No, I couldn't find any money for the bus," I replied, "so I walked it."

"What!?" she cried, horrified. "Oh that's nonsense! I left the money on the table!"

"Well I couldn't find any money on the table. It wasn't there!" I said.

"It's behind the vase!"

Knowing Mum, she'd probably put the money on the table and the vase on top of it, so if anyone else walked into the house, they wouldn't see it. But I didn't know that. Both Hilda and David were already there and if they'd taken it, they would have told her. Mum was actually very happy to see that I had arrived okay.

"Well, come on then, you're here now so you may as well enjoy the water."

The thing was, however, that when I had finally found them that afternoon, it was nearly time to go home! But I did get to play in the water for a little while, just in the shallow part of the waves up to my knees – I wasn't game to go out further because I knew I couldn't swim! Mum had also given me a blue bucket to play with and as it was a pebbly beach, I also got to put some interesting rocks in it. As soon as it was starting to get dark,

Mum called us back.

"Let's go home," she said.

When we got back to the house, Mum went to the big vase on the table.

"Here it is!" she said, picking it up and sliding out the coins, (about a tuppence or threepence worth, enough for the bus fare).

"Oh!" I replied.

"Silly Billy," she said. "You didn't think to look under here, did you?"

"No, I didn't!" I answered.

It might have helped if she'd left a note or something!

My family at Seaburn Beach.
From Left: Hilda, David, Brenda
Dad, Me (back of; age about 8 ½ years),
and Mum.

৪০৫৪

The Day I Nearly Drowned

An English canal.

A few months later in the school holidays, Mum and Dad rented a houseboat on the canal about an hour away from home for a week's holiday. It was just like a small boat with big windows, and a small deck at the back, where you boarded it to go through a small door to the inside. We had bunk beds up at the front end, which ran parallel to the side wall, and near the back of the boat, just inside of the little doorway, was the kitchen on the right-hand side, with a small lounge on the left.

The back deck had slatted planks which you could sit or lie on. My brother and sister had a great time lying on their stomachs and dangling their legs in the water. They held on by sticking their fingers in the grooves between the slats. I watched them catching the waves from the speed boats flying past us, and laughing away.

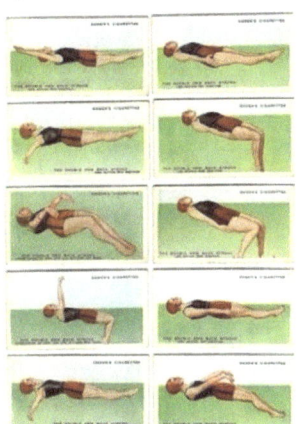

Then after a while they decided to go back inside, where Dad was getting all dressed up in a nice suit to go into the local pub for a drink.

I really wanted to give it a try, but I had never been in water before, and hadn't learnt how to swim. It did look like a lot of fun though. So I gathered up my courage and lay down on the deck on my stomach, feeling for the grooves to hold onto with my fingers, and dangling my short legs over the edge – and waited for the waves to come. I hadn't realised that my hands were much smaller than David and Hilda's, either. What I didn't expect was a boat coming very close to ours. It swerved so hard that it made the waves spring up and knock me clean off the deck!

Thankfully our boat was moored to the bank, otherwise I'd have been left behind in the current. Still, I knew I was in trouble. I went under, swallowing a mouthful of water and sinking quickly. It frightened me knowing that everyone was inside the boat while I was in the water, going down like a lead weight! No one knew about me! Boy, was I scared!

I felt my bottom hit the floor of the canal with a thud. Thankfully I floated straight back up, and I could see the sunlight shining through the surface. I remember thinking I'd be alright and as I got to the top, I instinctively opened my mouth for air, but got another mouthful of water and I went back under.

Again I hit the canal floor, laying there this time, wondering if I was going to die. Then I floated back up.

Just as I was going down for the third time, I caught a glimpse of a girl about my age, walking past on the bank. She must've been sent by God – I swear blind she must have been a Guardian Angel. If it hadn't been for her, I would not be here today.

She saw me and screamed out so loudly. I could hear her through the water, yelling that I was drowning. Next thing I knew, there was a big splash and my dad was coming in to get me. He must've flown out of the back door and without hesitation, jumped in – fully clothed.

As he pushed me up onto the deck, Dad quickly saw to reviving me. Mum came out about then, yet she must have thought we were playing a joke on her, for I heard her say, "Did you catch any fish for tea?"

Of course we weren't joking! It annoyed me that she had been so stupid as to say something like that! Obviously though, she wouldn't have known what had happened and she was trying to make light of it.

I'm just so grateful that Dad knew what to do, and that the girl on the bank was there before I went down for the last time to get his attention and save me! I never got to meet her, so I didn't learn what her name was.

But I was badly shaken, and Mum quickly dashed back in to get a towel as Dad brought me to the kitchen inside. Mum fussed over me with the towel, eager to get me dry; both of them were very worried about me.

"Go and lie down," she gently said after a while.

I went to my bed and tried to settle down, though it seemed ages until I felt safe enough to relax.

Dad ended up staying on the boat that evening to make sure I was okay. I think this experience brought us closer together and was why we stayed close in life too.

I never dangled my legs over the side again.

The next day Dad went to the pub, quite relieved to know that I wouldn't do that again. I just played inside the boat or on the ground outside in the local park. We enjoyed the rest of that week without incident before returning home.

And I was *very* happy to go home, too!

News 1948: Queen Elizabeth II gives birth to son, Charles.

Dad Leaves for Australia

When I turned nine, Dad sat us down to give us some concerning news...

"After Christmas, I will be going a long way from home," he said.

We waited, having no idea how far away, or why.

"I will be going to Australia!" he announced.

Us kids didn't know how to take it. Where was Australia? How long away from here was it? We knew it was another country but we really had no idea of the distance, much less anything else about it.

"But why?" we asked and, "When after Christmas?"

"I've got a job lined up," he said. "Here, it's in the local paper."

He showed us the ad in the newspaper; the Australian government was advertising for strong tradesmen to work in Australia on a new dam project, and they badly needed workers. Dad's brother might have given him the idea for it, I don't know,  but it was going to change the rest of our lives.

"I've applied for it and been accepted," he said. "When I get a home over there for us, I will send for you all."

I'm not sure how my brother and sisters took the news, and I don't

recall if I was too happy about it myself, but at the same time, I was sort of excited too. Australia! We were going to be going overseas! We were going to a place that had strange animals and warm climates!

But it wasn't now. It wasn't going to be for many months yet, and after he did leave, the days stretched out like it was forever without him at home.

Around two weeks after telling us this news, Dad invited some friends over for a Christmas party, and I was nominated to look after the record player. This was a big responsibility, for you couldn't scratch the records – and it was too easy to do that!

Whenever we had parties, on would go the records, and Mum and Dad used to let me stay up because I was the wind-up girl; I had to turn the handle when the record would start to slow down. I'd sit in a corner of the room on a tall chair beside the old gramophone. Dad would put the record on and it was my job to keep it going. It was fun and after the party had finished and the visitors went home, I went to bed very happy to have been included, for in those days, children were usually kept out of the adult's world, we were "seen but not heard". I was also happy because we'd been allowed to stay up so late!

***

Two weeks later, it was time for Dad to leave us. He was about to travel to Glasgow to board the ship called the *El Rancho*.

It was in mid-January 1950 and we were so miserable to see him go. He had hoped we would understand, but we were kids – how could we understand that an income was vital for living? How could we know just how expensive it was to raise a family of six? Jobs were scarce in Sunderland at the time and it was probably the case for many areas.

This was the era in Australia's history where they were looking to boost their economy and they decided to call out to 'the motherland' for new immigrants to help populate the country and contribute to the development of buildings and cities. They did this by offering migrants a free boat ride in, or what was otherwise called, "the Ten Pound Pom".

For ten pounds you could get a one-way trip to Australia, on the provision that you were coming to stay there permanently and become a citizen. Ten pounds was a lot of money back then. My Dad, for example, would have made only about fifteen pounds a week, twenty at the most.

Another incentive by the Australian government was to subsidise the cost, so that even though it was an expensive trip, it was cheaper going as a migrant labourer or tradesmen, (or family members of one) than going as a full-fare passenger on holiday. Lots of English families packed up and moved there, believing they could make a better life for themselves in the 'new country'. As far as I know, the Australian government paid the subsidiary for Mum and us kids to come out.

Well, the day finally came to say goodbye to Dad.

He left the front door, (that opened straight onto the footpath) and walked down the street, headed for the bus stop not far away. The bus would take him to the train station, which was only about ten minutes away, where he would get the steam train to Scotland. There, he'd board the ship that would take him to his new beginnings.

At the corner, he turned right and stopped to wave.

I waved back, wondering why we couldn't go and see him off on the train. No doubt it was because there were too many of us kids for Mum to manage, as well as the extra money it would have cost her to put us on the bus, and no doubt it would also have been more upsetting for us all.

It was the saddest thing to see him as he rounded the corner, giving us a wave and a smile. I don't even remember anybody else being there. Just me, and Dad, and that he was leaving. To me, he was only going from say, Sunderland to London – not all the way around to the other side of the world! I had no idea how far away Australia was, or how long it would take to get there.

I was teary. I think we all were. How long would it be until we saw him again?

***

The next twelve months were hard on Mum, she must have missed him terribly, and at times we all felt lonely. We too, missed Dad so very much. I missed seeing his smile, or hearing his voice. I really missed his jokes and the way we'd play tricks on the people.

Dad always had tricks on hand and he'd muck around with them whenever we had visitors. And one trick, one game he used to like playing was with a deck of cards.

"Would you like to see a magic trick?" he'd say. "You didn't know my daughter was psychic, did you?"

"No," they'd reply, curious.

"You wanna see a psychic trick?" He'd say again, calling me over. "Well okay, here's a deck of cards. Shuffle them."

He'd hand them the card deck and wait until they'd shuffled them, then take it back.

"Right," he'd continue, "I'm gonna put nine cards out, and you've got to touch one." He'd lay out nine cards, face down, in a three-by-three grid, and hold the rest in his hand. "She'll be out of the room and can't see you," he'd add, nodding his head to me to leave. "And when she comes back, she will tell you which one you've picked."

While I was out of sight, he'd tell them to pick a card from the grid. They only had to touch it, not pick it up or memorise it or anything. Then he'd call me back in.

When I'd return, he'd be smiling and say to me, "Now, which card did they pick?"

I'd take a look at the cards laying down, frowning, pretending I didn't know which card they'd picked. Sometimes I would point straight to it, and sometimes I would muck around and say, "Ooh this is a hard one." I was trying to make it funny for them.

But out the corner of my eye I'd check Dad's hand that was holding the rest of the deck. Where his thumb or finger rested, was the clue to the right answer. "I dunno, oh I can't remember," I'd add, frowning and pretending to think hard about it. Sometimes, for fun, I would point to a wrong one and say, "I like that one," and then I'd suddenly change with, "Hang on, ahh… Oh, I think it's this one!"

The visitors were always stunned and, even as I was saying, "this one", they'd be reacting with surprise.

"Oh, that's amazing!" they'd say, or, "Oh! How did you know?", or maybe even, "Wow she's clever!" or something like that.

And Dad would be smiling proudly and say, "she's psychic!"

And they really thought I was psychic back then. But they didn't know Dad had cleverly had his finger on the card in such a way that told me exactly which one in the layout had been picked. The irony to this story is that later in my life I really *did* become a psychic! I wrote about my experiences with Spirit in my early seventies in two books, *My Encounters with the Spirit World* and *Beautiful Spirits*.

Dad had had a fascination of being a magician one day, and he'd certainly had a bit of a magician in him. Among his things were the big rings that could magically loop together.

How do they work?" I'd asked him one day.

"Well, you just rattle them backwards and forwards, like this," he'd said, showing me, with the right sort of jiggling, how the loops could be interlinked or undone. "And… see that little groove?"

I could see this tiny weeny groove in the metal ring that he'd pointed out. "You gotta make sure they go into the groove there. They're easy to move."

With the knack he had, he made a motion and the rings were interlinked. "You always have to hold your hand over that so they won't see anything," he'd said. "There, from one ring to the other!"

One of his favourite things was the sarcophagus. Inside this tiny coffin was a purple mummy, fixed with a magnet and a spring. He'd say something like, "Abracadabra, wake up!" Secretly he'd give it a tap and the little mummy would pop up. Then he'd say, "Abracadabra, go to sleep!" and like magic, it would go back in! It doesn't spring back up these days, but I do still have it.

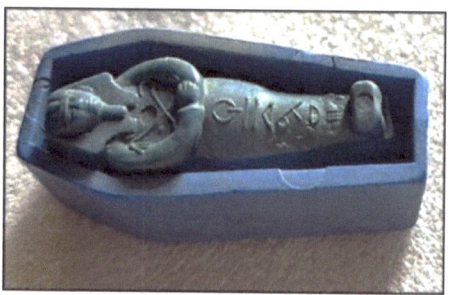

My Dad's 'magic' mummy.

He used to have a lot of fun with his magic tricks, but the card trick was the only one I was allowed to join in with. We got on well for that, because I always went along with whatever he'd said was right. But as for Mum, I think she was jealous.

෴

Moving Overseas

My tenth birthday came and we got great news from Dad. He not only had a home for us, but we were going to Australia right after New Year on a big ship!

WOW! What a surprise!

We were all excited and I couldn't get to school quick enough to tell my teacher and good friends.

The next few weeks seemed to take forever. I began to think it was all a big joke. Near Christmas itself, we were told to go to our local doctor to have our needles – that's when it all began to sink in.

It was true. We were finally going to go away!

But I had no idea just how far Australia really was...

***

From Left: Me, David, and Hilda. Taken before leaving home.

Poor Mum had a big job ahead of her. She had to sell off all of the furniture and sort out all of our beautiful toys that we treasured, to either give them away or sell what she could. Then she had to do all of the packing of what was left. We helped where we could but I don't think I helped as much as I could – for that, I now feel sorry, for the many times I have moved in my lifetime – with my kids, too – I know how hard it is, and therefore, how hard it must've been for Mum with four kids in tow!

It was now January 1951 and two nights before we left home, there was a circus in town. As a last treat, Mum took us along, and we had seats in the wing. I remember seeing the elephants doing their tricks, and the horses prancing around the ring with all the pretty ostrich feathers coming out of their heads. There were trapeze artists, and wild lions, that came out and roared and jumped through hoops.

We were one of the last to leave the big tent when the show was finished and we saw the horses being taken out too. We got on what I think must have been the last bus and, being a double-decker, we were up on the top deck, right up the front. As it pulled away, we saw the horses being walked away, perhaps to a nearby paddock, and people were already starting to pull the tents down.

It was a great night and we enjoyed every bit of it.

The next day Mum bundled us into a taxi and we went up to my Aunty Lena's house in Springwell, about fifteen minutes away. Mum's sisters, her brother, and all of their kids were there to say goodbye in a farewell get-together meal. What a party it was!

That night, Mum called a taxi to take us to the local station to catch the train to Glasgow. Grandma Hollywood, my favourite grandmother, was there to see us off. Just as we were getting into the taxi at the side of the road, she gave me a big hug.

"Goodbye Sweetheart," she said.

I noticed tears in her eyes.

"Don't cry Grandma," silly me said, not realising just how far we were moving to. "I will see you again one day! And I will come back and visit you whenever I can when I get older!"

"Yes Darling," she said. I'm sure poor Grandma knew differently.

"Bye Grandma. Love you!" I said, and climbed into the taxi, thinking we were only going to be a 'stone's throw' from the mainland (or the distance from say, Australia's mainland to Tasmania – something not very far away). As far as I was concerned, I was going to be coming back, and it wasn't going to be that hard to do so, either.

My beautiful Grandma Hollywood; the only picture that I have of her, which is from a copy of a photograph.

So I waved to her with a big smile, fully expecting to return to her soon enough. It must have been harder for Mum, for she would've known the kind of distance we were about to take.

But it was the last time I would see any of them again, apart from my Aunty Alice, who came out to Australia in the mid-seventies, (much later in 2015, I met my cousin Irene and her kids when I finally got to revisit them in Sunderland). Of course, I didn't know this back then. Years later I wondered if Grandma knew it was to be the last time she'd see her daughter and us grandkids. Mum was her 'baby' of the children, and they were pretty close. Whenever she could, Grandma would come around to look after us; she loved it. Mum was rather close to all of her sisters, too. Grandma and my Aunty Maude were two people I would miss the most.

***

Around ten p.m. the steam train arrived to take us to Glasgow. We all climbed into the carriage, which was of the very old-fashioned style usually seen in Agatha Christie or Miss Marple shows. There was the narrow corridor down one side, with sections of little cubicles that had bench seats facing each other. Once we'd settled into our compartment, Mum told us to lie down and try to get some sleep, because it was going to be a very long ride.

I remember waking up a couple of times, looking up at the night sky, seeing the clouds in the moonlight; it was fascinating. I also remember looking up at Mum a few times. She was very sad, and had tears running down her cheeks.

It's quite possible she doubted if she would see her family ever again, or at least, probably not for a very long time.

ৎ০০৪

The S.S. Cameronia

As the night wore on and the train chuffed along the tracks, my siblings slept, but I kept worrying about Mum, not really knowing how she felt or what she was thinking. I know she didn't get much sleep. The trip seemed to go on forever, like we were never going to get to our destination. I even thought the driver might be lost, silly me!

But as the sky faded into early morning light, Mum told us to wake up and get ready, because it wouldn't be long before we arrived at the station. Then at last we pulled into Glasgow. Boy, was I glad to get off that train!

We made our way by bus for a short drive to the docks. It was weird though, because the bus stopped at this very large shed. I was expecting a huge wharf, and seeing the water and boats, not realising that our ship was actually waiting on the opposite side of this shed – everything was so new and exciting!

Mum made sure we were all together as we got off the bus, then we made our way into the big shed, where two large doors were blocking us from seeing the dock itself. She had to fill out paper work before we were allowed to get on board, and paid ten pounds each for the four of us. It seemed to take a long while. It was noisy and busy, and the January draft was cold.

When we did go through those doors, we were immediately faced with this *enormous* ship! I had never seen such a big ship before and I was still wondering where *our* boat was that was going to take us off the mainland to this island called Australia, nearby. I was amazed by the size of it.

Mum carried Brenda and told David and Hilda to keep an eye on me, and to hold my hand going up the gangplank. I think she was worried that I might go too close to the edge and she didn't want me to fall off. That's when I realised that we weren't travelling on some small boat, but we were in fact boarding *that* ship, the *SS Cameronia*. Our journey would be its maiden voyage to Australia, after having served time in the war for the troops. We were its last passengers before it was to be decommissioned within about five years' time.

As we approached the end of the gangplank and stepped onto the deck, the staff were waiting to show people to their cabins. It was all so new to me and I was simply bewildered. We were taken to our small but comfy room, which had six bunk beds, a small cupboard and a toilet with a small hand basin.

After we got settled in, I decided to go and explore our area. I went around every corridor, found the public bathrooms and play room, and even the very large dining room. Boy was I surprised at the size of it! There were tables everywhere, set for over one hundred people, I'm sure. I remember thinking, *'these people have gone to a lot of trouble for what's going to be a short journey!'*

I told Mum about it later.

"It's not a short journey we are going on," she said, "because it's going to take us six weeks to get to Australia!"

What a shock it was to me. How could it take that long? The longest any trip I'd been on had taken was the day's bus ride to Nottingham, and the long train ride from Sunderland to Glasgow the previous night! Nothing had ever been so far as to take more than a month to get to! Soon I was to find out what six weeks travel was really like – and just how far, far, far away this new country was from home.

An example of the route of our ship.

As it was approaching midday, the captain announced that if anyone wanted some dinner, it would be served in the dining room within the half hour, and to please make our way there now. In England, our three main meals of the day are called breakfast, dinner and tea, (in Australia, it is called breakfast, lunch and dinner. This was a confusing thing for me when growing up!).

We went down to the dining room and were served the kids' meal – a three-course meal! First there was soup, then the main meal, then sweets (Australian term is *dessert*). It was the same amount of serves at every meal time – a three-course meal, three times a day – and it was too much for me. I was only used to having *one* set of three courses of food at lunchtime in school! But I ate most of it most of the time, for I was brought up not to waste food – not ever!

In fact, it was drummed into us, "Eat all of your vegies or you won't get sweets!" Of course, kids love sweets, don't they? And we so badly wanted whatever after-tea treat was coming, that we forced those overcooked, awful sprouts, beans or broccoli down, even when it made us feel so fat we thought we would burst – or be sick! I think, too, that we were made to eat everything on the plate because food was scarce during the war, and no one was looked on kindly if they left anything; you were considered as being wasteful.

The ship's meals were *very* filling.

Towards nine p.m., the announcement came through that we were about to leave the shores of England. If anyone wished to wave goodbye to their family or loved ones, then please make their way to the deck now. This was a sight I have never forgotten, and will never forget as long as I live.

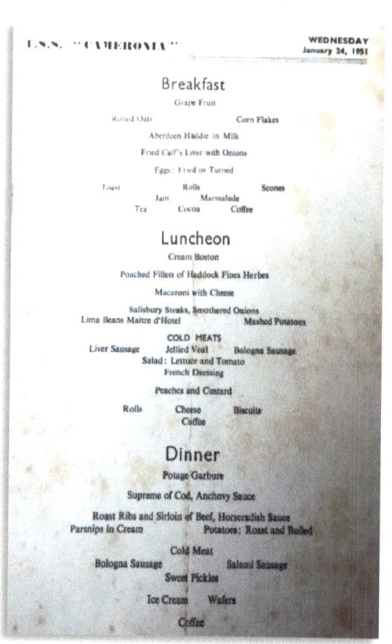

We raced up to the deck.

A menu from the ship.

As the engines started to roar, we slowly pulled away from the dock, where all the lights there seemed to go very bright, like a Christmas tree. People waved to each other, some smiling, some crying. We had no one to wave to in particular, but it was fun to wave anyway, and to pretend we were somebody important farewelling a nation.

As we moved further away, the lights appeared to lose their brightness, and the coastline got smaller and smaller until they looked almost like fairy lights. Then they seemed to all go out together. It was magical to me!

Then we went down to our beds.

***

The next morning, it was back down to the dining room for breakfast, and a new day on the big seas. We sailed for a long time before seeing any land again. I played in the kids' play room and wandered the decks, being very careful to not get too close to the railing. It was fun, and after a while we saw large fishes jumping in and out of the water. People said they were flying fish, but they were probably dolphins or whales, because they were a long way from the ship.

We travelled for around a week when, out of the blue, we saw land in the distance. As we got closer and closer, it became clearer to see the workers there, using picks and shovels on the shore. It was the Suez Canal, and it was fascinating to see these dark-skinned men stop to wave to us as we passed. It felt almost as if we could touch them, they were that close!

Then in the distance, we saw what appeared to be the tops of the pyramids. Although they were a long way off, they were still visible to us. As the boat made its way slowly through the canal, we saw dwellings and what appeared to be shops of some kind. It was all new to me and I was intrigued by everything. Then it was all gone.

After leaving the canal we went back to the big ocean. Another week went by and another announcement came.

"Attention passengers. If you are interested in seeing the biggest rock in the world, it will be coming up soon."

This, of course, was the Rock of Gibraltar.

WOW, he wasn't kidding!

The Rock of Gibraltar.

I thought it was only going to be the size of a big house, or maybe a double-storey building. But no, I could barely see the top of it as we passed by. It was huge! This felt even closer to us than the workers on the canal. I was sure we could reach out and touch it. In my head, it must have been as tall as the Empire State Building, or maybe the Eifel Tower (not that I had seen either of them to compare it with). But it was great to see it.

***

When we left the area, it was back to the large seas and it took us another week to arrive in the Columbian waters. The announcement came that the local natives would be coming out to meet us on board to sell their wares. As the ship couldn't dock in the port, so they had to come to us in their small boats, much like a fishing boat.

The locals clambered up the stairs on the side of the ship and bombarded us with all kinds of hand-made craft, clothing and jewellery. One man came up to Mum and I with colourful beads. I liked a lot of it and hoped Mum would let me have something.

"Pick something out that you like," she said and gave me some money.

I looked over everything, amazed with it all. My eyes were drawn to a necklace of alternating yellow and white teeth.

"Shark tooth! Shark tooth!" the man said in his broken English dialect.

I thought that it couldn't have been real shark's teeth because I assumed they'd be much bigger. To me, these had to have been something like cat's teeth.

The man was insistent. "You buy! Shark tooth!

I looked at Mum, really wanting the necklace.

"If you want it, you can buy it," she urged.

I loved it, and smiled and nodded, handing over the money (I don't remember how much it was). I wore it often, thrilled with the fascinating blend of white and yellow teeth around my neck. I'd had it for many years, too, wearing it now and again as an adult until the string finally broke. But I couldn't throw it out and I kept it wrapped up in a box, taking it with me to Western Australia with my own family in 1984, where it eventually went missing.

The natives were on board for around two hours, wandering the decks back and forth to sell as much as they could before slowly returning to their boats. Mum ended up with a beautiful scarf, though I don't know if David or Hilda got anything themselves.

***

Our journey moved on towards the equator.

When ships cross over the equator, they often have a centuries' old tradition called the *Line-crossing ceremony*. Sometimes commercial passenger ships call it *Baptism on the Line*, or *Equatorial Baptism*, and the Navy call it *Crossing the Line*. It's supposed to be a type of initiation ritual for passengers and crew who haven't crossed the equator before, and features the Roman god of the sea, King Neptune.

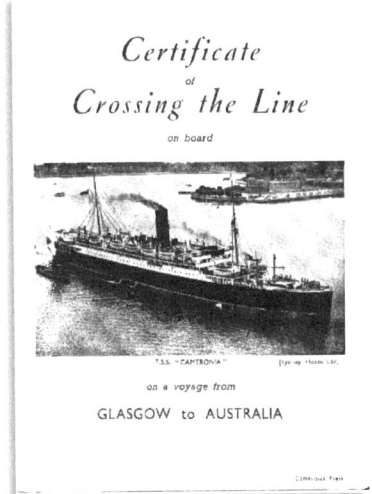

On our ship, a man was picked to play the king, and he was put on a plank of wood that had rope tied at the sides and hung from a crane of some sort. It was fun to watch him get lifted up over the ship's swimming pool, with the audience cheering him on the higher he went. When he was dangling high enough above the water for some five minutes, the wooden seat tilted backwards, dropping him with a huge splash. Everyone roared with laughter and we all got to celebrate with a big party after that.

***

The next day was a children's dress up party, where all kids up to the age of fifteen were allowed to enter a competition for the best costume. Mum had made friends with a lovely lady earlier on in this trip and she had taken a shine to me. She wanted to dress me as a sunflower.

She bought a lot of dark green crêpe paper and some dark yellow crêpe paper and went to town cutting the corners off the yellow paper, then sticking it to a very small hoop that fitted my face. She then wrapped the green paper around my body and arms to look like leaves, and placed the hoop onto my face.

"There!" she said. "You look like a beautiful sunflower now!"

A group of around two or three dozen children lined up on the deck, all dressed in fancy costumes! Some music was started and we all paraded into the hall, where passengers and the competition's judges waited. As I went past their stand, they all smiled at me as though I had a chance at winning, but it probably was because I looked cute, who knows. Maybe they did that to all the kids?

Unfortunately I didn't win, but had apparently come close. It was between me and another child for third place, which he got. But it was fun dressing up.

***

Memories From My Past

A few nights later we were told there was going to be a film night on the ship's bow. Unlike today's cruises, movies weren't screened every day, and we certainly didn't have television on board! So, after tea, when it was just on dusk, a lot of people went along to see it. Mum allowed us kids to go providing David and Hilda kept an eye on me, though she didn't come with us.

So we marched on up there too, excited to watch a free movie with the grown-ups.

I remember everybody was lying down either on the deck or on reclining chairs, looking up at the big screen, waiting for it to start. In the front of the deck of the bow, there was a very large square hut-type of thing – I think that was called the hatch, I'm not sure, but it was only about a foot high and you could sit up against the wall at the back of it. We made our way to it and clambered on top, with lucky me in the middle of David and Hilda.

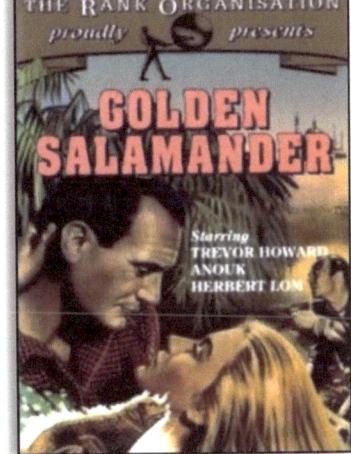

All movies back then were in black and white, of course; we didn't know what colour film was! This one was called, *"The Golden Salamander"*, with Trevor Howard, Anouk Aimee and Herbert Lom. It was exciting to see the screen light up and the music start.

Because we were still in the region of the equator, the night was stinking hot and I started to feel tired. By the end of the movie, we looked around and saw that most of the people were sound asleep, snoring their heads off. It seemed that they were allowed to sleep on the deck if they wanted.

"Do you want to have a sleep up here?" David asked us.

"Yeah alright," I said, and we curled up and went to sleep.

Early the next morning I stirred and saw the sun coming up over the horizon.

'*Ooh that's shiny!*' I thought, closing my eyes because its light was blaring in them.

I turned around and expected to see my brother and sister and at least some other people still there. I got a big fright, because nobody could be seen. I was the only one on the deck!

That's when I realised how frighteningly close to the side of the ship I was.

The hatch was perhaps within five or six metres of the railing, which didn't have the extra rows of safety bars in it like modern day cruise ships. And I was small enough to fit through them. I could feel the boat gently rocking on the waves...

My mind raced – what if the ship had encountered rough seas? If it had listed, I could have rolled off the hatch, onto the deck and out over the side, and nobody would have seen me?

David and Hilda must have woken during the night and gone down to bed. Whatever time that was, I'd had no idea. But they hadn't bothered to ask me to go with them, and they were supposed to be looking after me! Not even one of the crew, or the adults who had been up to watch the movie, had woken me up to say, "Hey, wake up little one. You've got to go down to your cabin – there's nobody up here!" There was usually always somebody walking around, wasn't there?

But nobody whatsoever was on the actual deck where I was.

'*They're all probably down in the kitchen getting their darn breakfast ready!'* I thought angrily. So I jumped off the hatch, made my way down the walkway, found a door, went through it – staggering along the corridor with the rocky ride – and found a way all the way down to our cabin, what felt to be at the bottom of the biscuit jar. I walked in and Mum met me with a surprised look in her eyes.

"What are you doing up so early?" she asked. "Where have you been?"

I told her what had happened.

"What!?" she exclaimed. She took one look at David and Hilda – they were out like a light. "Do you know what time it is?" she asked, horrified. "Nearly half past six! You're not to do that again!"

She was so angry, though from my experiences of being a mum later on, I suppose it was probably because she was so worried about my safety. I don't remember her going mad on David or Hilda because I went to bed straight away, going off to sleep again with what bit of cool air we had from the fan in the wall. But I think she must have had a go at them, as they'd said that they couldn't wake me up, and that because there were other people around, (still sleeping) they thought that I would be okay.

Nevertheless, we were never allowed to sleep on the deck ever again. I woke up in time to still have breakfast.

೫೦೧೩

Memories From My Past

Australia

Australian Waters

About five days later, we were informed that we were to enter the Australian waters near Fremantle, Western Australia. If anyone wished to embark to the mainland, they had to wait at the doorway to the stairs at the side of the ship. Due to there being no port for the ship to pull in to, they had to anchor off shore, and then passengers were taken in small, ferry-like boats the rest of the way. Mum took my little sister Brenda and I up to the child care room, where we would stay while she went across to Fremantle city. As far as I know, David and Hilda stayed on the ship too.

I was allowed to watch her go down the steps and onto the ferry-boat, and kept watching it as it sailed to the mainland, then I returned to the child care room. Apparently there was a talent quest going on and as I entered the room, I heard the voice of what I thought was an angel. She was singing *Somewhere Over the Rainbow*. I thought Judy Garland had come on board!

When I went in and saw the singer, I realised it wasn't Judy Garland, but a beautiful young girl. So I waited to see if she would win. I watched the contestants going through their routines and hoping that she came first, because I was so taken by her voice.

After about an hour, the winner was announced. The young girl did indeed win the competition! I was very excited to hear it and soon went to be with Brenda. Some two to three hours must have passed when, just as I was settling down to play with my little sister, Mum walked in the room. I was pleased to see her.

"I've bought some things at the markets," she said. We went down to our cabin, where she showed us the exciting things she'd bought.

After dinner we were off again. It took another week to arrive in our next port; Melbourne. Up until now on this long journey, I had thought it was funny to see people rushing to the side of the ship and throwing up, usually straight after eating. I thought there must have been something wrong with them, or that they weren't healthy. But after we went through the Great Australian Bight and round the southern Victorian coastline, I learned why.

The waters had become very choppy. The ship was tossing and pitching and I was frightened, because I thought we were going to drown. Water came up over the bow every time we pitched. I had had my dinner and now it was my turn to be sick. Boy was I glad when we eventually got through that awful section and my tummy was able to settle!

About three days later, during mid-morning, we arrived in Melbourne, Victoria. Half of the passengers got off there. It was eerie after that – hardly anyone around, and you particularly noticed that in the dining room at meal times. That same night, we set off again, this time bound for Sydney, N.S.W., our final destination. It was another week at sea.

I thought we were never going to get off this ship! But seeing the harbour lights again was good. It was so beautiful and made the trip more relaxing. At last, three days later, we arrived in Sydney Harbour. It was around midday; our things were packed, Mum checked that nothing was left behind, and she had us up on the top floor in a corridor, where a big line of people were also waiting to disembark. Boy was I glad to be finally getting off that ship! At least now I understood why Mum said it was going to be a *very long* trip – she really meant it!

While we were waiting in the corridor near the door with the gangplank, I saw this man come up to Mum and give her a great big hug. It was eerie seeing him hugging her and then David and Hilda.

'*Who is this stranger hugging Mum?*' I thought. '*And she doesn't mind!*'

It wasn't Dad, in my opinion, because he looked different to this man; he had a much rounder face and had put on weight.

He turned to give me a hug too.

"Joyce!" he cried, wrapping his arms around me.

That feeling of those arms was very familiar. It was the way my father used to hug me back home in England. I knew this had to be Dad and realised that his rounder face and tummy must've been due to eating well.

When everyone had been greeted, he said with a big smile, "Come on, let's get you off the ship! I've got lots to show you all!"

༄༅

Castor Oil

As we made our way down the gangplank and into the big shed on the dock, Dad told us that we were going to stay at a friend's place for perhaps a couple of weeks, as our new house was not quite ready to move into yet. When Mum and Dad had seen to the paper-work with customs, we were on our way.

Dad had his friend waiting outside to drive us to his place in the suburbs of North Sydney. In those days, we didn't have seat belts and the cars were typically bench seats in both the front and back. Even though people were allowed to have small children sit on passenger's knees, we were cramped into his car like sardines.

He was a very nice man, but boy, if I only knew then what his wife was like – I would've turned around and got back on the ship!

She seemed to be a very nice old lady, on arrival; it was at dinner time that we kids were to learn about her strict views. We were shown to our rooms and given a chance to settle in, then early that evening, we were told to sit down at the table so she could serve up our meals.

"You have got to eat it all up," Mrs. Benson said, bustling about. "It will make you strong. And if you don't eat it all up, you will get a spoonful of castor oil!"

I looked at Mum, not knowing what castor oil was. I'd never heard of it before, and why did we need it? Also, what would it do for us in place of not eating all of our food?

Mum indicated to me to at least try and eat it all, but unfortunately it was a big meal and I couldn't finish all of it. Plus we were fresh off the ship, and still adjusting to a different type of diet! We were all given far too much on our plates. My older sister, Hilda, refused to eat all of her dinner because like me, she was full.

Guess what, the lady wasn't joking!

She frowned at the left-overs and went back to the kitchen, and came back with a bottle and large spoon.

"Open up!" she said to Hilda.

Reluctantly Hilda opened her mouth.

The lady put the spoon into her mouth, holding it high so that every last drop went in.

"There you are!" she said, looking smart.

Hilda pulled a face and shivered, then she ran into the bathroom where she threw up. Us kids looked at each other, terrified we would get the same treatment. I forced myself to eat some more, but it was just too much. So the lady made me have the oil too! Yuck! I *hated* it!

This was to be a ritual at every meal. If we didn't eat everything that she gave us the castor oil is what we got. I think I got this horrible stuff more than once or twice, and my brother David got it a few times, yuk! And each time, we threw up. Obviously the failure of the oil's trick went unnoticed, or perhaps it didn't sink in that we weren't going to eat what she gave us despite being threatened with the oil! I guess Mum or Dad didn't want to say anything to her out of politeness to their hosts, but geeze I wish they had!

We hated her after that.

One day around three in the afternoon, Dad, in his wisdom, decided to take us into the city to see the sights. Us kids couldn't get away from her quickly enough. Getting back to her place near tea time, though, was heart breaking, and we dragged our feet in the door, wishing we didn't have to see her. But at least Dad was able to say that we weren't hungry because we had already eaten in town.

Luna Park circa 1950

On another day, he decided to take us to Luna Park, which was great fun, because we had never been to anything like that before.

On both occasions you could see she wasn't very happy with him, but he couldn't care less. Good old Dad, he had come to our rescue!

One morning she gave us lots of soft little orange-brown things for breakfast. They were covered with an orange sauce, and served on two slices of buttered toast, (real butter back then, not margarine). It looked horrible, a bit like something an animal had thrown up.

"What's it called?" I asked her.

"It's called Baked Beans, and it is good for you," she replied haughtily. "They gave it to the soldiers in the army for their strength, and they survived, okay?"

'*I hope so,*' I thought, looking at my plate. '*I dread having more castor oil!*'

To my surprise, I loved them.

But Hilda didn't and she couldn't eat much of them, so guess what?

That's right, she was given more oil, poor thing!

I asked if I could have it again some other morning.

Two days later, she gave us two fried eggs, two slices of bacon, and more baked beans on two slices of toast. I ate the lot!

But Hilda left the beans.

So she got more oil.

I think that lady enjoyed giving us that horrible stuff just to see our faces change. But we managed to get through the second week albeit with difficulty. Then the news came – great news that we had been waiting for.

Dad came into the room this particular morning, smiling with excitement.

"We can leave tomorrow," he said. "Our new home is ready for us to move into. The government has checked to see that everything is in place, and the people in charge have said it's fine – it's ready for us to move into immediately!"

Yay! The government had saved the day!

We were overjoyed and couldn't wait to get out of this lady's house quickly enough. I think we all slept very well that night.

Early the next morning after breakfast, we packed all of our stuff into the boot of the man's car, and crammed ourselves in the seats like sardines again. Then we headed for Sydney's Central Station to catch the steam train to a place called Penrith. We didn't care how squashed-in we felt, or how long that drive seemed to take, just as long as we were going away from that lady! No more bloody castor oil!

We arrived at the station about twenty minutes later, piling out of the car and eager to get to the platform. Dad and Mum collected our luggage, thanked the lovely man, and said goodbye. Then we headed for the ten o'clock train.

ಲಿಂ

The Long Ride West

When the train arrived, we got on, full of excitement. These carriages were different to those in England. They still looked much like they do in the movies, but instead of cubicles on one side and a narrow corridor on the other, these had bench seats facing each other, with the aisle for walking down the middle. You could fit six people on one side and four on the other.

Locomotive 5801 brings a South Coast goods train into Sutherland station.

We found an empty pair of seats and sat down, and since David and Hilda had boarded before Brenda and I, they were the lucky ones to get the window. About ten minutes later, everyone who was travelling on this train was seated, ready to go. And we were off!

"Get comfortable," Dad said, knowing what a long day this would be. "It will take about four hours to get to Penrith, and another two hours or so by bus before we can get to Warragamba."

None of us really knew just how long this trip was going be – or how big this new land actually was. We had only Dad's word. Four hours might seem like a long time in today's world, but steam trains were slow and only chugged along compared to diesel and electric-run trains. We really had no idea how big this country was. At the time though, we didn't mind. We were simply excited to get away from that nasty lady in Sydney. After we had travelled for around thirty minutes, we began to wonder when we would arrive at this place called Penrith. I was thinking back to poor Grandma Hollywood and was concerned about us ever visiting her again; it was just so far away!

***

The trip seemed to go on for hours – seemingly more than the expected four – and I was worrying if we'd even get there before tea time. Hopefully we wouldn't miss the connecting bus to our new home!

Eventually we arrived at Penrith at about three-thirty that afternoon. The connecting bus arrived at three-forty-five. It took another hour to get us to a place called Warragamba Dam, where we were going to live; our final stop. Yi-ha! At long last!

Our bus drove into a very small town, with just a row of shops of about two dozen businesses, from a paper shop to a butcher's, a milk bar and café, even a hairdresser's! Plus a pub. Every town had a pub. The bus stopped outside of this small General Store, that had a house attached at the side and towards the back of the building. The long, very, *very* long journey had finally come to an end, almost.

Fortunately Dad knew the people who owned the store and they were expecting us. We walked down the little path to their side door, avoiding the shop itself as it was just

The main road in Warragamba town; the General Store (far right).

on closing time. They were happy to see us and showed us all into their living room, then proceeded to close the shop up for the night.

The lady offered us dinner. She was sympathetic and understanding and didn't demand we drink oil if we didn't eat all of our food! What a contrast she was to the lady in Sydney! Her husband was great too. When we had finished dinner, he offered to drive us to our new home. He even helped us to carry the luggage inside! We all got on very well with this couple and stayed friends with them for a very long time.

෪෬

Memories From My Past

Steps were on left side of the front verandah at the time

No garage at the time, but just a dirt driveway

Warragamba

Finally we had arrived at our new home! And oh, it was lovely, and very different to our English house!

Excitedly we explored this new place and were surprised to find we had proper, separate bedrooms! No more sharing with Mum and Dad! And David was thrilled to have a bedroom of his own! There was not only these three bedrooms, but a nice loungeroom, a kitchen, a separate small bathroom, and a laundry that led to a small wooden veranda out the back door. There was also an outdoor toilet just outside the back door!

In England, our house was joined together in one long row with the others, but this new house was separated from the neighbours – free-standing – with front, back and side yards that gave lots of space between them. Everything was

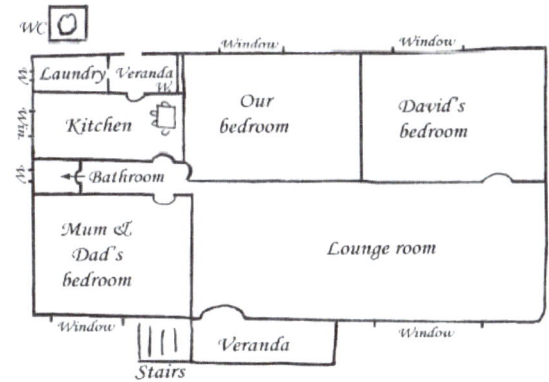

Above: My sketch floor plan of our house in Warragamba (as in 1951; not to scale).

more spacious here. It was terrific. This was living!

***

We soon settled into our new surroundings. The only thing we found that we didn't like was the heat. It was March, an Australian autumn, and we were not used to it. In fact, it took us five years to get adjusted to the Australian weather. I remember when the winter came; it was heavenly! We thought it was like our English summer and we were *still* feeling the heat!

Early one day, it had rained very heavily. My younger sister Brenda and I wanted to cool down, so we asked Mum if we could go and sit in the gutter to catch the recent rainfall. She agreed, so long as we put on our swimming costumes. Excitedly we did, and then ran down to the gutter out front of the house. It was deep enough to feel the water flowing around our bodies, and we enjoyed it running up our backs.

We had played there for about half an hour when the next-door neighbour, who possibly meant well, spotted us. She came out screaming to Mum.

"Hilda!" she yelled at the top of her voice. "*Hilda!* Get your kids out of there! They will catch their death of cold!"

But Mum just smiled at her.

"They will be okay," she calmly said. "Don't worry about them."

The lady looked horrified.

"Well then don't say I didn't warn you!" she retorted and went back indoors, very upset that Mum had ignored her.

She let us play a while longer, as we were quite happy and a lot cooler, then she took us inside, where she ran us a warm bath in an actual bath tub.

It was fascinating to us that she could pour both hot and cold water, together, out of taps that were fixed to the wall, for in England, making a bath was a very different thing, and lot of work. Our bathtub there was a very large tin tub, which sat in front of the open fireplace of the lounge room. Mum had to boil the household kettle on the iron grill about six times just to get enough water to fill the tub. By the time she'd had enough, the first lot of water went cool, so it was warm by the time we got in. One by one we washed and as each child got out, another one got in, using the same water, which needed topping up if it cooled too much!

But this purpose-made bath changed everything and boy what a difference it was! We could have a bath at any time, making the water hot or cool, and the older we got, we were allowed to have one on our own when we liked!

So after the bath on this particular evening, we got ready for bed, had dinner, and settled down in the loungeroom with Mum and Dad, listening to the radio, (for television hadn't come to Australia yet). We felt very relaxed and very happy, with not a hint of a head cold about us!

୧୦୯୨

Taken at home in our first year at Warragamba, (from left) Me, Hilda, Nellie, David and Brenda.

Australian Schooling

Shortly after moving in to our Warragamba house, it was time to start at our new schools. In England, once you got to fourth grade, high school was the next level you went to, and I had reached the end of fourth grade in Sunderland before we left. So I went with Mum when she took Brenda to the nearest public school, ready to put her into kindergarten. While there, she asked where the nearest high school was for me.

They asked what level I had reached in England, and Mum told them.

"On no," they said, "we have fifth grade and sixth grade first. *Then* high school. We have to assess her before we can decide what class to put her in!"

It didn't matter what we said, their answer was final, and for some reason, they made me repeat fourth grade for a few months, after which they let me move up into fifth grade. I'm not even sure if Brenda had been accepted into kindergarten either!

Naturally I was very disappointed. I had really wanted to go into high school, which was at Penrith!

It was a very long walk to get to the primary school too, with no busses to pick me up or take me back. So I went to *Warragamba Primary School* and I was reasonably happy there for most of the time, but the teacher I got, Mr. Goodman, wasn't nice. He made my life miserable and I didn't like him one bit. He was English-born too, and the way he spoke made him sound conceited.

Because I was a Geordie, I had a distinctively broad northern English accent, and it really annoyed him. He insisted that I start speaking *Australian* right away, and he'd get so angry whenever I said words "wrongly", yet his own way of speaking "Aussie" was just as bad!

The classic "Gidday" that Australian-raised people use was tricky for me, because "day" in Geordie is pronounced as "*dare*".

So I'd say, "Good-dare," in class, which always ruffled him up.

"It's not Good-dare," he would say in an awful, grumpy voice, while staring down at me with a stern face. He was a tall man and very arrogant. "You're in Australia now! It's Good-*dye*!"

I would cringe with embarrassment. He didn't have to be so loud and bossy about it. And the kids would laugh among themselves whenever I got into trouble. That's why I hated him in the end, because he was so mean and liked to humiliate me.

*My school class photo 5A 1952
(Me left, 11 ½ y.o. standing in
front of Mr. Goodman).*

૱ൡ

The Awful Alsatian

In August, six months after arriving in Australia, I turned eleven. Mum and Dad bought me a bicycle to ride to school. It was fun racing around on it and made going to places much quicker!

Around about this time, Mum took up with betting on the Saturday horse racing. In those days, parents regularly sent their kids off to the local pub to put their bets on. It's unheard of now, but quite normal back then. Now that I had my bike, it meant I could ride to the pub for Mum instead of walking there. I rode to the base of the steep hill, got off and pushed my bike halfway up, then crossed over the bush track to the hall. After placing her bets, I'd come home the same way, only flying down the hill instead. It was great fun, and I used to look forward to her sending me off to the hall just for the ride!

One day, just as I was coming up to the crest of the smaller hill, a very large Alsatian dog rushed out and attacked me. He'd jumped his owner's fence and bolted straight at me, knocking me clean off the bike. I rolled down the embankment opposite his house, and luckily a neighbour saw it happen. He ran down to help me, chasing the dog back to his home and screaming to the owner to tie him up.

I believe it was my lucky day, for that dog surely would have mauled me, if not killed me. This brave neighbour carried me back home. I was bleeding down my arms, leg and face. He took me inside where Mum cleaned me up, while he went back for my bike. My, we were so grateful! We saw him as being a good Samaritan.

The following weeks went by pretty quietly and I was back to walking to school again, until another neighbour offered to drive me there with her daughter. When my bike got fixed up, I rode very cautiously passed the house with the dog. Luckily he never jumped the fence again. I suppose that either the owner may have heightened it, or he kept the dog tied down.

ಬಿಂಛ

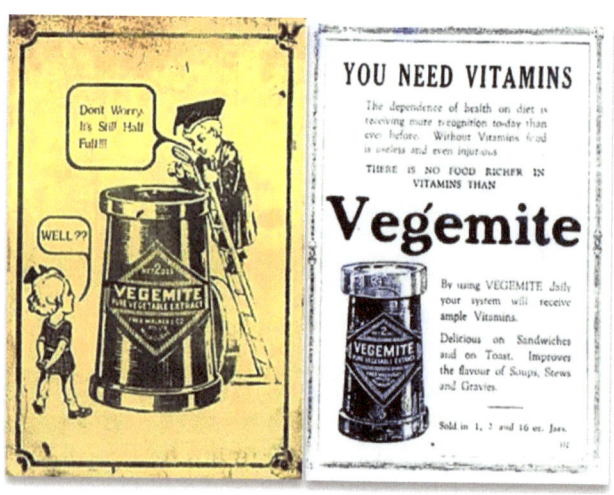

Running Away

In early November, Mum and Dad decided to go to our local picture house in the town centre. It was to be their first night out since we had arrived in Australia, treating themselves to a movie.

"Now, Joyce, Brenda," she said before going out the door, "I want you two to be good, because I'm leaving Hilda in charge of you."

About an hour after they left, Hilda found little things to start picking on me with, like telling me to stop making noise when turning the pages of my book, or talking too loudly to Brenda because it bothered her while she read her own paper or book.

I didn't think that I was being noisy or too loud, and her agitation with me escalated into a big argument. As far as she was concerned, *she* was right and I was wrong and she wouldn't let up. I got so upset that I ran into my room, crying.

When I saw her favourite bible on top of the dressing table, I grabbed it, and started ripping its pages. I was so cranky and so hurt that *I* was supposed to be the one at fault when *she'd* started it all! And when Mum would come home, she'd make me look really bad and I'd probably get into a lot of trouble!

I'd had enough. Hilda often picked on me and I came to the conclusion that there was only one way to deal with it. I was going to run away!

Me at around 11 y.o.

I took my favourite dress from the wardrobe and put it into my empty school suitcase, then quietly climbed out of the bedroom window. Thankfully none of them heard me and I secretly snuck away into the night without any of them knowing.

I walked up to the shopping centre with no idea where I would go, but I knew one thing – Mum and Dad should know what I was doing! I wanted to tell them I was running away and that they were not to worry about me!

So I went to the theatre house and up to the lady at the counter who sold the tickets and things.

"Can I go in to see my Mum and Dad please?" I asked her.

She was a bit surprised to see me.

"Why do you want to do that?" she asked.

"Because I need to let them know that I am running away."

Who knew what she thought, but she paged Mum and Dad by putting a message across the bottom of the screen, asking them to come to the foyer. Within five minutes they came out looking very worried.

"Joyce!" she cried. "What are you doing here?!"

"I'm running away," I said, trying to keep my tears in check.

"What?! Why?!" she asked, horrified.

"Hilda's been picking on me all night!" I began. "She kept telling me to be quiet, or to sit still or to stop talking so loudly to Brenda! She said it was annoying her!" This was my chance to get in before my mean sister could. "But I haven't been noisy, Mum! I was just trying to read my book!"

"Well that's no reason to run away!" she said.

"Yes it is! She's always picking on me, Mum!" My emotions took hold and I let rip. "She started things – like she always does – and then wants to blame me for it! It didn't matter what I said or did, *I* was in the wrong! Not Brenda, or David! Just me! It's always me! Well, I'm not taking it anymore! I can't! So I'm running away to be rid of her!"

Mum's face was frankly not amused. She grabbed my arm and turned me around while thanking the cashier, and she marched me off to the door with Dad.

"Let's go home and find out what really happened," she said angrily.

I could tell she wasn't very happy with me at all for spoiling her first night out with Dad.

Back at home, I knew Hilda would put all the blame on me, saying that I started the argument, so I was prepared for it. And the shock on her face as we walked in the front door was great to see. Her jaw dropped and her eyes flew open; her expression said it all. She obviously still didn't know I had taken off until now.

"Mum! Dad!" she yelled, startled. She didn't know what to say, and blurted, "Joyce!" when she saw me.

Mum's voice was firm.

"Okay, now what happened tonight for Joyce to run away?"

Hilda went straight into self-defence, blaming me for everything she could think of.

Mum looked at me with a stern eye, probably doubting me now.

"You go to bed," she said. "We'll discuss this in the morning." Then she turned to my mean, nasty sister. "*You* finish up what you're doing and you can also go to bed. I've had just about enough of you two!"

So off I went to our shared room, knowing Hilda slept in the same double bed as Brenda and I. My side was next to the window that I had climbed out of, and Hilda slept on the other side nearer to the bedroom door, while Brenda, being so small, slept in the middle of us. So I turned the light off and got into bed, and pretended to be asleep when Hilda finally came in – I wasn't going to give her the satisfaction of bullying me if she'd known I was still awake.

The next morning Mum sat us down and told us how upset we had made her and Dad feel. She said this was not to happen ever again and she gave Hilda a warning to try and have patience with me, or else she would be very angry with her.

'*Patience?*' I thought, '*How about telling her to stop being a Bossy Boots?!*'

She must have listened though, because she backed off after that and things were okay for a while.

Us kids at the Warragamba Park in 1952
From Top - down: David and Hilda 15 y.o.
Briane (a friend) 12 y.o.
Me 11 y.o., Brenda 5 y.o.

೫೦೦೩

The Black Doll

Four weeks before Christmas, Mum had bought us some presents and had also told me what she was going to give to Brenda, which she believed would be just what she'd want. On this particular afternoon though, Brenda was playing up like any four-year-old child does.

"If you are a good girl, Santa will bring you a beautiful black doll with pretty, long black plats," Mum said to her.

Brenda burst into tears and threw a tantrum.

"I don't want a black doll! I don't like black dolls!" she cried.

Mum frowned.

"Now what will I do?" she said quietly to herself. "I've spent a lot of money on it and I can't take it back now."

I followed Mum to the kitchen, wanting to let her know that I thought the doll would be a wonderful present to have.

"Don't worry, Mum," I quietly said. "I'll have her."

Mum seemed to think on it.

"Would you *really* like it?" she asked. "I thought she'd love a doll, seeing as how we don't have much at the moment. I didn't stop to think that she wouldn't like it."

"Yes!" I replied with a grin, knowing I would. "I'll quite happily take it, if that's okay with you. It's better than having the money go to waste."

She smiled and gave me a big hug.

"Thank you, dear," she replied, "that is a big relief."

Two weeks before Christmas I was still thinking about the doll Mum said I could have. I really wanted to see what she looked like and I searched everywhere for it when Mum wasn't around, but I couldn't find it.

"Where did you hide the doll, Mum?" I asked her as casually as possible one day.

"Why?" she asked.

"Oh, no reason, just curious," I muttered, and then I thought, a little white lie won't hurt. "I just wanted to know in case Brenda went looking for it, and I could stop her."

"Oh, don't worry, she won't find it," she replied. "It's on the top shelf in my wardrobe."

Well, now I knew where to look.

A couple of nights later, at around eight o'clock, I took my chances to get a sneaky peek at the doll. I waited until after the evening meal, when the family was distracted with listening to the radio, but what followed was an experience I've never forgotten in all my years since.

I snuck into Mum's bedroom and cheekily approached the wardrobe. It had a long mirror down the centre that reflected the front window of the house. Quietly I opened its door and reached up to the top shelf.

As I felt around for the doll, I became aware of this very bright light shining as if from *within* the mirror. I stopped and looked at that light, realising that I was seeing a God-like figure in there.

He had a moustache and beard, wore long white robes that were embroidered with gold and had a golden cord around his waist. And he was wearing a regal crown. I thought I was staring at God himself!

The wardrobe.

I froze, wondering if it was Jesus instead. Either way, I was frightened.

Our house was built onto the side of a sloping hill, with the backyard on the high ground, and the front, sloping down to the road. My parent's room, in the front of the house, was built on posts that were nearly six feet tall, and the empty space underneath the floor could have almost fitted another room down there.

Left: This picture of my brother David (about 14 ½ y.o.) and his friend, on the stairs at the then front of the house, is an indication of the gap between the floor and the ground.

So I knew no one could have been standing outside of their window because it was too high off the ground – yet this man in the mirror was in full view! I could see him from head to foot, not just the upper half, or just his head and shoulders.

Then I realised that I must have been seeing a reflection, so I quickly turned around to look at the window behind me.

True to form, the same, God-like man was there. He looked very sad, while slowly shaking his head in a 'no' fashion, and waving his index finger from side to side.

It was clear what he was saying to me, "That's not right."

I was caught out, and I looked back at the mirror; both the beautiful bright light or the man were in it now. But on looking back at the window – he was *still there*!

His sad expression didn't let up and I felt sickly inside knowing that I was being a naughty girl by trying to see this doll before Mum had a chance to give it to me properly, as a gift. So I closed the wardrobe door quickly and raced outside to check that no one was playing tricks on me.

It was perfectly quiet in the street below, and completely empty right outside of Mum and Dad's window. There was no one – *no one* whatsoever – hovering up there.

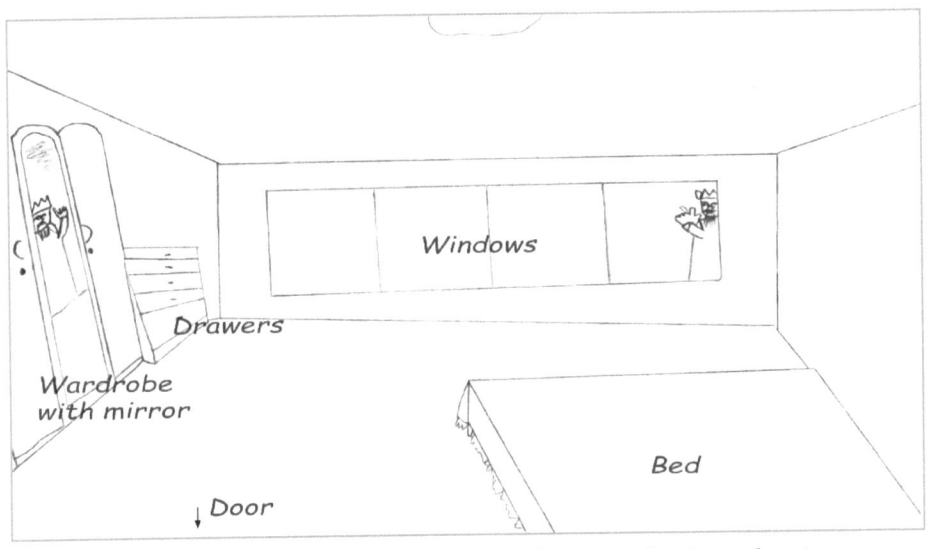

Above: My sketch of Mum and Dad's bedroom at the time, showing where the wardrobe was in relation to the front window (not to scale).

Feeling very confused, I returned to the door of Mum's bedroom, wanting to look in but not game enough to go all the way in there at the same time. Cautiously I opened it and peered across to the window.

And wouldn't you know it, that same God-like figure was there, hovering outside, and smiling at me!

It was incredible. Some would say it's unbelievable.

But I know what I saw that night. I know the impossibility of anyone dressing up as God and pretending to be levitating outside of that window.

I *know* I was given a very special encounter.

I took my cue to leave well enough alone. It was a warning, perhaps to spare me from getting into trouble with Mum, or perhaps to save me from something worse, like falling backwards and having the wardrobe crash down upon me, who knows?

Christmas Day couldn't come soon enough.

When Mum finally gave me my present, I hurriedly unwrapped it, and boy was I glad I had waited. She was beautiful! My face must have said it all, as Mum was more excited than me to know that I really did adore her. She's still with me more than sixty years on.

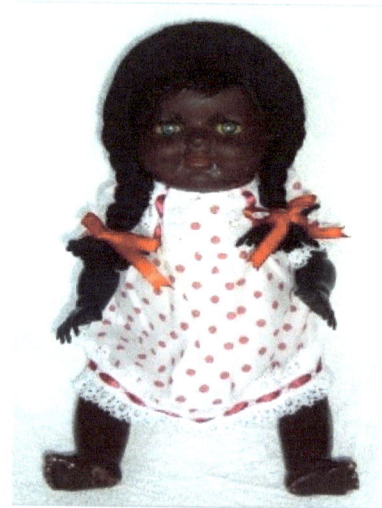

My black doll (with new hair and dress).

ಏಲ

Otford

Just after Christmas 1952, Dad was in Sydney, walking up the big, long stairs near the city's Olympic Pool and Luna Park, when he met his second cousin coming down the stairs, who recognised him. I guess they mustn't have seen each other in a long while, because they got on talking, and Dad must have told him where we were living.

News 1952: King George VI dies.

"Well if you want a better place," his cousin had said, "I can get you a better one. And you can get more money in Sydney; you can get a better job."

"Alright," Dad had replied. In his time working at the dam, he'd seen several really bad accidents, and some of them had been of men who had fallen to their deaths. The labour was also very hard on them, a physically demanding job, so I suppose he'd have been keen to leave it.

"The only thing is, your wife might have to be a caretaker for this mission thing."

"Where abouts?" Dad had asked.

"Otford."

Dad jumped at it. We'd been living at Warragamba for nearly two years when he'd resigned from his job at the dam, and now in 1953 we were off again to a new place. If it hadn't been for Dad meeting his second cousin in Sydney, we probably would've still been in Warragamba, and looking back at it now, I know he'd made a bad move.

We were happy as a family there, only Dad had thought, 'better job, better money'.

But he didn't look at the place first. And it *was* in a desolate area! It ended up being a nightmare for us. Luckily the place was going to be rent-free, which was no doubt what had helped them make the decision to move there.

***

Mum's new job was as a care-taker to a dual-built hall and large shed that was owned by a church, and it was situated on a gentle slope almost directly across from the train station, which was about a hundred metres from the end of our driveway.

Back then, there was nothing in that area but farms and a small village a couple of kilometres away from the hall, and lots of surrounding bushland. The train was the only way to, or from, this out-of-the-way place if you didn't have a car, which we didn't yet. Otherwise there was just a narrow dirt road to the village.

When we got off at the station this day, with all of our luggage, Dad led the way forward. We had to go down a bush track to a little embankment, across a little creek, and then up a slight hill into the driveway – this would be our shortcut whenever we went on the train, rather than walking to the road that led up to the station from the village.

Otford Station (partial view).

Our house at Otford, (the shed on the far right built after we'd left).

The new 'house' was a large fibro shed, which was roughly the size of a small, single-car garage (that was later to be seen in the 1970's). All that was inside it was a dividing wall, like a T-junction shape, and that helped break up the one, big room into two small bedrooms at the far end, and the 'family room' for the rest of the shed.

It was very disappointing. Our Warragamba house was a mansion compared to this dingy little box.

Mum put my brother in one of the small rooms, and us girls in the other one, while she and Dad had to have their bed in the middle of the loungeroom! They used their

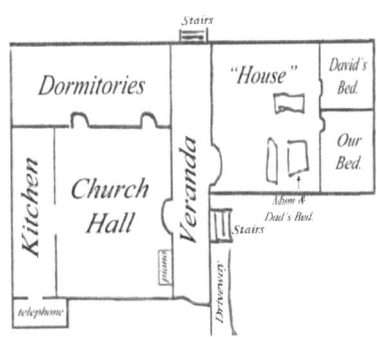

Above: My sketch floor plan of our house in Otford (in 1952/3; not to scale).

wardrobe as a kind of other wall between their bed and the shed's door, which helped to separate it from the front of the building. They sat the lounge along the side of their bed; around the corner from the wardrobe was the pokey kitchen and dining area.

There was no bathroom or toilet inside. Mum had to have a metal bucket on hand in the space we called a 'lounge room' – a distance of maybe three metres from her bed! There was a tin can "dunny" available to the campers on the other side of the hall from us, but we were allowed to use it only when they were not there. And besides, I was scared there was Redback spiders in there too! And snakes!

The tin can dunny was literally a tin can, that was often placed under a wooden seat, or bench, (with a large hole in it for sitting on). Typically strips of newspaper or old telephone books were used for toilet paper. The can was emptied once a week by men, who carried it to a truck for disposal into giant pits.

***

We learned very quickly that the farmers that lived around the corner didn't have fences to keep their cattle in, and their animals were always around us. More than once we would come across them in the dark, their big wet noses in our face or the huge pats of smelly poo on our feet. So we couldn't even go to the toilet of a night time in case there was a bloody cow out there!

It was shocking, and I don't think Mum was happy with that either. I know *we* weren't happy with it!

A narrow wooden veranda separated our 'house' from the church's hall, which was much bigger than our tiny shed, and its main entrance was diagonally across from our front door. The hall had a piano in the corner, a separate kitchen down the back, with a little side room for the old wind-up telephone, and on the right-hand side was the dormitories for the church-goers. Separate to all of this was the small shed split into a toilet and laundry, where the washing was done. I think there was a shower in that shed too. The church campers arrived every Friday night around six o'clock and left on the Sunday after an early breakfast and service.

Well, first thing Monday morning, poor Mum had to go into that hall and clean it. She had to wash the floor, clean the telephone down, wipe the piano down, clean up the kitchen, making sure everything was spotless, including the dormitories and the back washroom and toilet. She had a week's worth of work to be done every time the campers went.

Boy it was tough on her! She was working bloody hard for them and I think she hated it, and sadly, she couldn't get anyone to do her own housework. Dad was working in Sydney, David and Hilda had just started jobs too, and I was going to school with my little sister, Brenda. So there was nobody left to help her, and we didn't know anyone well enough in the village to ask for their help either.

***

Otford was such a small place that the only road in or out of there was narrow and ended down at a weir not far from the bottom of our driveway. It had very few street lights, and maybe about a dozen houses and a general store up on the hill that went over the train line. Across the train line and just down from the store was a small school, whose principal was also its only teacher.

Aerial view showing part of Otford village Ca. 1948.

My spelling book at Otford.

When Mum enrolled Brenda and I in the beginning of 1953, there was about twenty kids all together: four kids in the kindy section, six kids in first class, five in the second, four in third and fourth grades, one boy and one girl in fifth class and two boys in sixth grade. When I had finished at Warragamba, I was leaving sixth grade, and I had been expecting to go to high school at Penrith.

But the principal of this school had other ideas.

"No, you can't go to high school until I've assessed you," he said.

I protested, saying that I had already been put back a year at Warragamba.

"I'll still need to assess you to see what you know," he insisted, and decided to put me back in with the sixth graders anyway.

I was devastated! I was looking forward to going up in classes and I couldn't understand why he made me repeat it. The constant repeating delayed my educational development and was very irritating!

***

We took the short cut to school each day, walking down the long driveway, turning right at the bottom onto the narrow dirt road towards the township, and crossing the weir's bridge there. David went swimming in this weir one day – and came out very quickly, covered with these rotten leeches! My poor mum had to pull them off with our help. I felt so sorry for her, and for my brother! It must have been awful!

On the other side of the bridge, half way along this dirt road, we would turn left on to a grassy path, that often-had ticks in it, especially in summer. I think it must've worried Mum a lot, because Brenda had got quite a lot of them in her head and in those days, we didn't have any medical treatments for them. A bite from a paralysis tick could put you in hospital!

Right: My sketch of our house's location to Otford village (in 1952/3; not to scale).

The path crossed the railway line, where we had to make sure there were no trains coming before stepping on the rails. It could have been dangerous if we were not listening carefully, because even steam locomotives, coming front-on, could be quiet if they didn't blow their whistle. Thankfully we had learned how to keep watch for them. We then climbed a wooden A-frame step ladder over a barbed wire fence into the paddock that the school house was built on. When it was wet, that part of the paddock became very muddy and we kids called it the pig-sty.

After school, we would make our way back home the same way, having to watch out for the afternoon trains as well.

We weren't used to the cows, the leeches, the ticks, the snakes and spiders, or the hike through the bush and it would usually take us about thirty minutes to walk. But and it would have taken us much longer to go up through the village, on to the hill and down around to the school. This was life in the Australian country!

☙❦

A lot of Bull

Time went by with no change to our daily routines, until one day my brother had a run-in with one of the locals... he was coming up from the station, and we could hear him screaming out.

"Mum! Mum! Hold the door open!" he yelled. "MUM!"

We looked out the door to see what all the commotion was about.

He was nearly halfway up the driveway, running as fast as he could, with a terrified look on his face.

About twenty feet behind him was a big, black bull, looking very dangerous as it chased him!

We opened the door right away.

I'd never seen such fear on his face and as fast as he ran, the faster the bull ran, catching him up in no time.

As David reached the veranda, he skipped the few steps and ran for the door. As did the bull...

Mum quickly shut the door behind my brother.

The next thing we heard was the *thump* of the bull as he head-butted the other side of it.

David tried to catch his breath.

Thump-thump-thump-thump!

We were scared, not knowing if the beast would smash it in. He was snorting and stamping angrily, unwilling to let the fight go. The rage in this animal could have killed him!

Thump-thump-thump-thump!

It seemed to go on and on.

We looked at the clock – Dad was due home in half an hour.

"What are we going to do?" someone asked. "What if it's still out there when Dad comes home? It might want to chase him too!"

"I need to get to the telephone," Mum said, "to ask the operator to contact the farmer next door. It's him who owns it!"

"He needs to be told that his bull is dangerous!" David snapped. "He ought to shoot it and give us some of the meat for our troubles!"

We were all fed up with how the farmer's cattle kept wandering onto our paddock as they pleased, and this had gone too far!

Fifteen minutes went by as we worried about Dad's fate on coming up the driveway; finally the bull wandered off some fifty metres away.

We were in luck. Mum made a bold dash across the veranda to the hall, racing for the telephone in case the big beast returned. She managed to get hold of the operator, who alerted the farmer to get his bull back as quickly as possible.

The type of telephone Mum had.

Within ten minutes the farmer came round on his motorbike and herded the animal back to his farm, just as we heard the whistle of Dad's train pulling into the station. It was such a relief!

"Phew!" we sighed. Boy were we glad to see the back of that bull!

"Oh thank goodness you're safe!" we cried as Dad came into the house, "David got chased by an angry bull on his way up from the station!"

"What!?" he shouted.

We told him all about it. Dad was really angry with the way things had been going, but he was glad we were all okay.

༄༅༅

A Pain in the Bum

The bush life with its creepy crawlies, the smelly cows, angry bulls, the feeling of isolation, and the hard, hard slog Mum had to go through week after week without Dad, David or Hilda there to help much, put a dampener on everything.

But things seemed to go alright for us after the incident with the bull. By November my principal told me I could go on to high school. I was thirteen! At last I would get to catch up with the older kids. Boy I was happy with that news!

Then the village Christmas Party came...

The parents put on a great spread of lovely food in the school's hall. Everyone was there, including my family and we had a great time. After the food was all gone, the dancing started. Mum loved dancing, I remember how she really enjoyed the party scene and getting up on the floor to dance.

Most of the kids went out onto the veranda though, under the bright party lights strung around the front of the building, and eventually about four of us made our way to the back of the hall, where it was mostly dark apart from the overhead light by the back door. Under this light was a set of wooden stairs that weren't fixed to the veranda, and because of recent rainfall, they had been turned backwards, so that the planks were upside-down.

But I couldn't see that they were backwards, and I was wearing shoes that had slippery souls. This is where it all went wrong for Mum again. I foolishly followed the kids down the steps.

On the fourth step, I slipped.

I came down with a terrible *thud* on the last two, screaming out and crying with pain.

A couple of the kids ran back into the hall to tell my parents what had happened. They came straight away and tried to pick me up, but I was in too much agony. I couldn't stand, let alone walk, and it was now I realised something was terribly wrong.

Dad was going to carry me home, as there were no doctors or hospitals in the area. We would've had to go to the next suburb to find medical help, and that was about half an hour's drive by car. So he gathered me up, when one of the parents who lived in the village said he would go and fetch his old car and drive us home.

But I was in so much pain that I couldn't even sit down, and I had to kneel on the seat, facing the back, instead. He drove as carefully as he could and when we got to our house, Dad carried me inside and gently put me on the bed. He planned to take me to the nearest doctor in Helensburgh by train straight after breakfast. Mum tried to help me change into my nightgown, and then I had difficulty getting into a pain-free position so I could sleep. The only comfy spot was on my tummy, but I was still in agony most of the night.

The next morning Mum helped me get dressed to go to the doctors. Still in pain, she then helped me hobble to the station. How I got there is a mystery, but I made it and when I got on the train, I had to kneel the whole time, gripping the back of the seat and whimpering all the way. About twenty minutes later, at Helensburgh station, a bus was waiting to take people to the town centre. I hobbled to the bus and again, knelt on the seat with my arms over the back rest. The ride was unbearable.

We managed to find a doctor who could see me soon after arriving at the surgery. Mum had told the receptionist what had happened so she could ask the doctor if he could see me as soon as possible. We only had to wait about five minutes when he called us in.

I explained the accident to him and he said it sounded like I had a broken tail bone. So with Mum's help, I was put onto the patient bed, where the doctor examined my back and lower spine. He put his finger inside my bottom, reaching up toward the tail bone, and indeed, found it was broken. It was very uncomfortable at the time but I trusted that he knew what he was doing. Soon enough, he put it back in place and asked me to try and stand up very slowly.

I did, and for the first time, I actually had very little pain! Though I was still quite sore, I could stand, and even walk a little better! We thanked him and left, slowly making our way to the bus stop to return to the station. Mum even dropped in to a shop and bought me a soft cushion to sit on for the trip home! The last thing the doctor said was, "Rest it for two weeks, then take it very slowly."

As it was now the school holidays, this made it very easy to rest up. I'm sure Mum was relieved as well.

But my fall was to be the last straw for us there.

When we got back home, I noticed Dad had a newspaper in his hand and when Mum was ready, they went through it together. I didn't know what they were looking for then, but I soon found out.

൸Ꮹ

The Half-House

Dad must have decided that he and Mum had had enough of living in the Otford place. Just after Christmas 1953, Dad gave us the good news; we were moving again! He and Mum had been looking to rent another house far away from this hell-hole. He'd found an ad in the paper, saying, "To Rent: Half a House" and it promised to be a good home with three bedrooms. Like hell it did. But we were now going to a place called Epping.

News 1953: Sir Winston Churchill dies.

The full house was owned by a lady who lived in a small building to the side of it. She'd split her house in half to make a duplex, and a husband and wife lived in the other side to the half we had. As it turned out, it was an old house, with our half really only having one small bedroom.

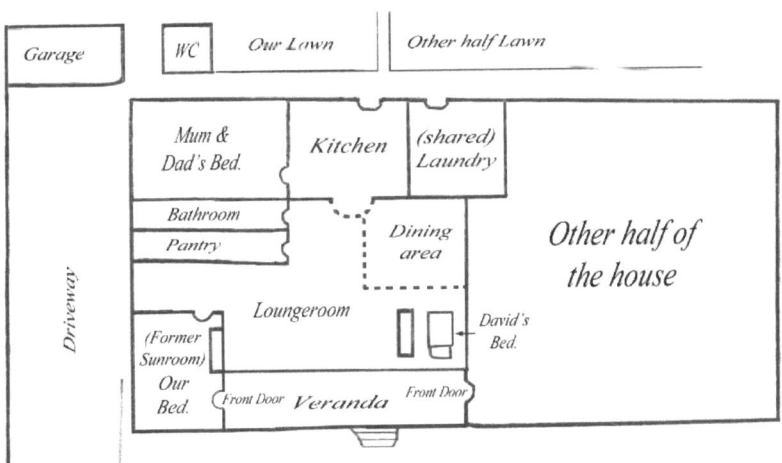

Above: My sketch floor plan of our house in Epping (in 1953; not to scale).

Memories From My Past

What would have been the main entrance into a sunroom (off the front veranda), had been turned into a second 'bedroom'. It was about the size of a typical bathroom, which my sisters and I got to sleep in – but it was also still the main entrance for family and visitors!

We had double bunk beds, with Hilda taking the single bunk on the top and Brenda and I sharing the bottom bed. It was a bit squishy, as we were growing older now and were not so small as we were in the previous houses.

Then there was a nice big loungeroom off this room, which spanned the width of our house-half. David got to have his bed stuffed in the corner of it, right near the front and dividing walls! Mum put up a wardrobe for him to act as a third wall to give him some level of privacy, but his feet faced straight into the dining room, and if visitors were at the table there, they could see him! So he had to wait until everyone was finished and gone home before he could go to bed. And we three girls couldn't go to bed either as they had to walk through our room – right passed our beds – to leave!

Opposite the dining room was a walk-in pantry beside a narrow bathroom. Then there was the 'master' bedroom at the very back of the house, which was barely the size of a double bed! They had just enough space for a small wardrobe and chest of drawers. Even the adjoining kitchen was bigger than their room!

Mum had to go out the back door from here to access the community-style laundry, and she had to share the washing

machine and clothes line with the next-door neighbour, just as Dad had to share the outside garage with her husband. Even the yard was divided into two by a concrete path down the middle, and we all had to share the outside dunny as well!

We thought this whole set up was bloody ridiculous! It was advertised wrongly. It wasn't *two* houses in one, it was literally one house with a wall down the middle! But it was still better than Otford, and by the time we were moving in, my tail bone had healed really well.

Though there were discomforts, Epping was a nice township not far from us, and we had a bus stop just up the hill to take us there, so everything was handy. So we made do with living here for about a year and a half.

The only trouble came when Mum enrolled me into school again. She had taken Brenda to the local primary school and while there, she made enquiries about the high schools that were near to us.

"What age is she?" the principal asked her.

"She's just turned thirteen," Mum said. "She's just left sixth grade at Otford and is due to go to Sutherland High School."

"We will have to assess her before she goes to high school," he said.

And guess what? I was put back into sixth grade for assessment *again*, and it lasted for the rest of the year! I was so disappointed. By now I was *really* looking forward to attending high school. They put Brenda back in first class, too! Each time we moved and I started a new school, I was put back a grade, and the constant changes meant I struggled to learn things like English and Maths.

***

After we'd settled in and Dad, David and Hilda had all started new jobs, Dad took driving lessons and bought his first car. It was an old bomb. A dark blue Morris Hillman, about 1936 or '46 model. He wanted to see more of Australia and whenever we could, we did a lot of travelling in it, including going out on family picnics and sight-seeing tourist places. Later in the year he even drove us to Queensland, to visit some friends who had come out to Australia on the same ships with us.

As it had turned out, Mr. 'Nocha' Round had come out from Leeds on the same ship, the *El Rancho*, with Dad in 1950, and also worked on Warragamba Dam with him. His wife, Edna Round, and their two kids Peter and Pam, came out with Mum and us four kids in 1951. She'd even had the cabin opposite us!

However Nocha didn't like Dad's driving and he'd close his eyes when in the passenger seat.

Being Cinderella

I did eventually manage to get into high school the following year – at the age of fourteen. I was sent to Hornsby High School, which was by bus and train, but I didn't like it because the kids in my year were younger and seemed to look at me as if I was weird. They didn't associate with me and I was pretty much on my own all the time.

I was only there for about three months, and then, because I had a bike and could ride to school, I wanted to go to Carlingford High, the closest school to us. So I was able to get a transfer there. It was a lot better, and I enjoyed being there. I learned how to cook and sew.

Four months later I turned fifteen. It's quite possible that because I was now learning the basics of cooking, Mum decided that I could help out with making dinner. As soon as I'd get home from school, I'd have to make sure the house was clean, then I'd have to prepare the vegetables for everyone's meals. When she came home from work, she would dish up the food, and afterwards, I would have to clean off the table, and wash up. For some reason she began to turn mean.

I remember one night I was quite tired and wanted someone to share the washing up with me.

"Can Hilda help me out and give me a hand?" I asked.

She was horrified.

"No she can't!" she roared in a loud voice. "She's been working hard all day! Now just get into it and shut up!"

'So had I been working hard all day!' I thought, but it was no use saying so if I wanted to avoid further argument. But Brenda was home, and probably playing with her dolls. She was old enough to put in some effort around the house, surely she could get off her lazy bum and help me?

"What about Brenda?" I asked.

Mum was furious. You'd think I was asking her to wash the dishes!

"Don't be silly! She's only a baby!" she screamed. "She can't do anything! Now shut up and get on with it! I don't want to hear anymore from you!"

Brenda was nine – *that* was still a baby!?

***

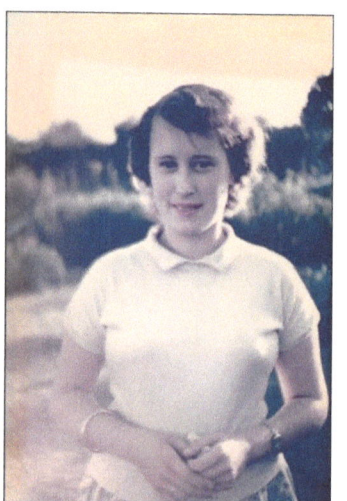

Me at 15 y.o.

Not long after turning fifteen, Mum had to go into hospital. Presumably she had been to her doctor and was given the bad news that she had to have a hysterectomy. This may have been the reason for her recent change of mood, but I didn't know that back then.

She didn't say anything at the time to me about feeling sick, or that she'd even visited the doctor. I only knew that she had to have this operation. But it meant one thing - that I had to leave school. She told me I wouldn't have time for lessons now as I'd have to run the house while she was away, and then I'd also have to look after her when she came home.

We were only a week out from the end of term and my cooking teacher begged me not to leave. She thought I had been doing so well and she tried to encourage me to leave at the end of the year instead. Even my algebra teacher said I was doing really well – and I didn't understand what algebra was! Apparently I was doing quite a lot better at it than most of the other kids.

But Mum was having none of it.

"Well I'll need you here,' she'd said. "I need you to help me around the house. After my operation I won't be allowed to do any heavy lifting!"

So I had no choice, I had to leave school – the only school I had actually enjoyed being at. And I'd have to do her heavy lifting on top of the housework!

Right back from our infancy, we kids were taught to obey our elders no matter how strict they might be, and if we didn't, or if we argued about it, we got belted. Over the coming weeks the whole half-house of

work fell to me. I had to vacuum, mop the floor, dust the furnishings, wash the clothes, hang them out, iron or fold them when dry and put them away. I had to peel the vegies, cook the meals and clean up afterwards. I couldn't go to bed until the kitchen and dining room were tidy, with everything put back where it belonged. And this is how my days went on.

When Mum came home from hospital about two weeks later, something had changed. *She* had changed. She seemed to be always cranky. She could go off at the smallest thing very quickly, and then she'd go on about it for hours or even days later. I thought it was because she was uncomfortable or in a lot of pain.

I couldn't do anything right and sometimes I'd cop a smack. Her temper was fierce and her hand could be hard. Smacks could be to my arm, back or head – whatever was closest, I guess. There were lots of times I would go to bed covered in bruises, crying, praying like mad for God to make her stop hitting me.

This is where I began to think Mum hated me, and I started to hate her. It seemed that *I* had to do *everything* by myself, because no one else was able to help me. Hilda was "too busy doing real work", (and couldn't do anything wrong by Mum anyway) and Brenda was "too young". Housework was "women's business", so my brother David, being a boy, wasn't going to be allowed to help me at all!

His job was to help Dad with "men's work" out in the yard on the weekends, like mowing or household and car repairs – although even then, I was asked to mow around the clothesline area when it would grow too quickly during the weekdays. I didn't

An example of the type of push mower we had.

mind the mowing, which was with the wooden-framed old style rotary wheel blade mower – no petrol-driven models back then!

Mum treated me like Cinderella and it didn't matter what I did, or how I did it, I couldn't please her. And of course, since she'd been off work herself, the family was not earning as much as it had. So I then went looking for work to help out with the bills.

I worked in two different Milk Bars not far from home, but only lasted a week at each because I was too short to reach the bottom of the freezers for the ice-creams. It was disappointing, but it was great to get the little brown envelope with my name on it at the end of the week. Inside was the money I'd worked hard for – my first real pay. I was so happy. But, it didn't last long…

When I got home that evening, Mum held out her hand.

"Let's see what you've got," she said. "And give it to me."

Although I was a little taken aback, I obeyed.

She took out the notes and coins, probably counting it in her mind to see how much I had earned.

"Good," she said and put the notes into her purse. She gave me the few odd coins back. "You can have that to go look for more work."

I was stunned. That was *my* money! I didn't know how to handle the situation and I didn't dare ask her for any of it back, afraid that if I did, she would belt me for it. This became the normal. Each week on pay day, she would wait expectantly for me to give her my wages, keeping the notes and letting me have the small change for bus or train tickets. She did the same with Dad, David and Hilda. If I wanted to buy something like clothes or shoes, it came out of her purse, and she would come with me to make sure I got something decent with it.

It's only now I wonder if some of that money was going on the horses! As far as I know, she'd kept gambling on them over the years, although after the hysterectomy, I think she didn't do it each week as she used to. After the first two jobs, I tried working in a factory that made jeans. It took me two bus rides to get there, and I had only been at the factory for about two months when Mum got some bad news from England. Her mother had passed away.

My beautiful grandma, the woman I cherished and had always thought I would get to see at least once more, was now gone. My chances of talking to her, seeing her wonderful smile or hugging her would never happen again.

Poor Mum. She was beside herself. She couldn't go back for the funeral, either. She had no money to spare for it, and I suppose in her mind, she also felt that she couldn't leave her husband and kids back here. This must have been the last straw for her, because she turned really weird. She got depressed rather easily and she'd have unpredictable mood swings.

She must have hated Dad for 'dragging her out' to this hot, fly-blown country on the other side of the world. Her anger became worse than ever, and she took it out on me. She turned quite nasty and I seemed to get the blame for everything that went wrong.

ఠఁౘ

Clive

Around this time I joined a youth group. My sister Hilda had already been going to it and she was getting to know a young man there, called Allan. I wasn't game to get too close to any boys because of Mum's attitude, although there was one boy, Kenny, who I had a school girl crush on, (and who I learned had liked the girls!). One night the group were having a slide night and I asked Mum if I could go too.

Clive (second from right) with mates.

"Yes," she said. "I want you to keep an eye on Hilda for me."

So I got to act as a chaperone for her, making sure that she didn't get up to any "fancy business".

Allan and his friend, Clive, brought some slides along of plants and wildlife, and Clive gave a commentary on them. Clive was a very nice, quiet young man and he tried to give a good explanation for each scene, but when a photograph of flowers appeared, he simply said, "Flowers". A few slides on and there was a picture of just one flower.

"A flower," Clive said, and everyone laughed.

I'm not sure if he was embarrassed, but I felt sorry for him.

After the presentation had finished, I went up to him to apologise for everyone laughing at him.

"That's alright," he said with a little smile.

We were both shy and I was nervous, too. He was rather handsome and I liked him a lot. He must have liked me, too, for we seemed to hit it off quite well. I found out that he and Allan were best friends since school, and that Hilda and Allan were seeing each other as girlfriend and boyfriend.

It was lovely meeting Clive and I kept thinking about him after we got home that night and in the coming days. I almost couldn't wait for the youth group's next gathering a week later. I smiled shyly at him when I saw him and as soon as we had the chance, we caught up and talked some more.

He must have really liked me because a couple of weeks later, he came to see me and we went for a walk. We came to a sheltered bus stop where we sat down and talked.

"Now, I'm going to go to Mt. Kuring-gai tomorrow to see my girlfriend," he said. "I want to see where we stand with each other. If she wants me, I'll come back and let you know. If she doesn't want me, will you have me back?"

One of our social groups. Right/lower: me (peach); Left Bottom: Hilda.

"You please yourself," I replied in a caring manner. "It's your life, you do what you like with it."

"You won't mind?" he asked.

"I've never really had you," I said. "As far as I'm concerned, that's up to you. Whatever will be, will be."

There were no misgivings as far as I was concerned. If that's what he wanted, he was welcome to it. So he went to her house the following evening and knocked on the door. Her mother answered and told him that her daughter, Robin, wasn't in, and that she didn't know where she'd gone.

But as he was walking back to the station, he heard a lot of laughter coming from a particular car. He looked in the window, only to see Robin in the back seat with three or four men, "playing around". So he decided there and then that he didn't want any part of being with her.

The next night he saw me, and we found our quiet place to talk back in the sheltered bus stop.

"Would you take me back, Joyce?" he asked.

"Well, you never left, really," I replied. "Why? What's happened?"

"I've called it quits with her," he said, looking hurt. "After what I saw, I want nothing do with her. She's been two-timing me. I don't want to see her anymore." He took my hand and added, "But if you're happy with me, I'll be your boyfriend for you."

"If you want me," I said, gently smiling, "I'll have you."

From then on, we started seeing each other a lot more. Whenever Hilda and Allan went out, I was allowed to go with them, secretly getting to know Clive. When we'd get to our destination, like say, the zoo, they'd go one way and we'd go another. Where I was supposed to be watching over Hilda, no one was watching over me. Clive and I grew fonder of each other and Mum didn't know a thing about it! She actually did me a favour by making me go with Hilda.

Left: Taronga Zoo, Sydney, taken by Hilda's then-boyfriend, Allan. From Left to Right: Hilda, Brenda, Clive and Me (around 16 y.o.).

Eventually she did learn of our budding relationship, which made her upset, of course.

"Don't get involved with him," she said, "he's an Australian. I want you to meet a nice English man!"

"But he *is* nice!" I protested. "He doesn't gamble or swear, and he's kind."

"I don't care. I want you to meet an English man," she insisted.

"He doesn't drink, either," I added, determined to hold on to him, "and that makes him good enough to keep."

We defied her anyway, and she sort of objected to me going out with him, but she didn't know that we had been already getting to know each other all this time.

ഌଓ

News 1955: World renown scientist Dr. Albert Einstein dies.

Out of Control Mother

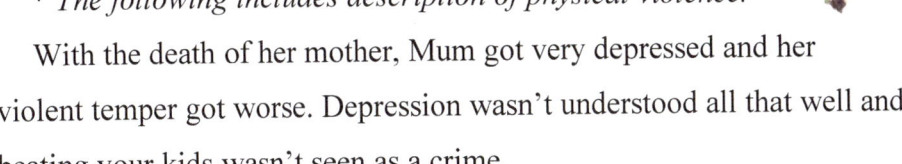

* *The following includes description of physical violence.*

With the death of her mother, Mum got very depressed and her violent temper got worse. Depression wasn't understood all that well and beating your kids wasn't seen as a crime.

One evening I must've said something to upset her again, because the next thing I knew, I was on the concrete kitchen floor, with Mum sitting on my chest with her hands on each side of my head, gripping it hard, bashing it up and down on the ground.

I was screaming for her to stop but she didn't. She was like a wild, ferocious animal giving me absolute hell. Her face was red – what I could see of it through my tears – and it was twisted with rage. It was terrifying. I had no knowing what I had done that was so wrong, nor any reason why bashing my head until it hurt was justified punishment. My brain was seeing stars when my beautiful, brave brother dashed in to help.

Somehow he dragged Mum off me, swinging her up against the back door with his left hand on her throat and his right hand in a tight fist, ready to hit her.

"Stop it!" he yelled. "Leave her alone or I'll hit you!"

Mum must have been scared stiff. She screamed at the top of her voice for Dad.

"Dave! Help! Dave! Come and stop your son! He's going to kill me!"

Dad rushed in, not knowing what she'd done to me, but angrily he grabbed my brother and threw him into their small bedroom just off the kitchen. He slammed the door hard behind him. Poor David didn't get a chance to defend himself. Dad must have pulled his trousers down because the next thing I heard was Dad's belt hitting his skin.

Whack! Whack! Whack!

He didn't stop. The sound was sickening. Every blow was severe and very soon David was screaming with pain.

I felt really bad because I couldn't help him. Mum was standing over me, glaring at me with mean eyes, her hand grabbing my arm so tightly it hurt.

"Now look what trouble you've caused!" she screamed. "Go to bed and don't come out! I've just about had enough of you for tonight!"

I was stunned. How could she put all of that blame on me? It was a miracle she hadn't killed me! If David hadn't have stepped in, she would have cracked my head open. How wrong was I to have copped all of that?

But I didn't understand any of that on that night. It wasn't in me to stand up to her, we kids weren't allowed to be defiant to our elders! I really hated her at this stage and it would be many, many years for the hatred to heal.

Left: David playing to an audience (about 15 y.o.)

My poor brother. I heard him sobbing most of the night. I felt so sad for him, and guilty about what she had done to me to cause him to get a ruthless strapping. He was nineteen, almost a man, yet he was treated like he'd been a very bad

Right: David (about 18 y.o.) and Dad having a beer.

boy when in fact he'd been my saviour. I wasn't game to go and give him a cuddle, to say "thank you for helping me", just in case Mum came out and saw me. Then it would have been on for young and old all over again!

That experience has never left me. Even to this day it haunts me. I was just so hurt and so terribly ashamed. I don't think she ever did tell them why she beat me so hard.

So you might think, *'Why was she taking it out on me?'*

When writing this book, I knew the awful experiences were part of my life too, but I couldn't understand why I had to put the bad stuff in. I didn't want to put Mum down as being a bad person. She wasn't always like that.

And one day I heard Mum's voice (in spirit) say, "You've got to put it down, because there'll be people in your same boat, and they'll understand why *their* parents were like that."

"*Well, okay,*" I thought. '*I have to put how bad Mum was and how she bashed my head against the concrete floor… and my brother saved me, and all of this is in the book.*'

And I got a picture of it in my head… I sort of put myself in her shoes – Mum not only had to come out and leave her mother behind, but she also left *all* her family behind. She couldn't just go around the corner to someone's house and say, '*I think I'll have a cup of tea with Maude…*' (or whoever), '*and they couldn't come to us,*'. And vice-versa, different things were happening out here, with the many moves, the heat, the bush life and heavy work in Otford, the ups and downs of running a family, Mum going to hospital, and then, her Mum dying and she couldn't go to the funeral. Her hysterectomy must have changed her personality, too. It would have had an effect on her hormones.

Looking back on it all, she picked on me for a reason, and it was because I *think* she didn't know who she could turn to; she didn't want to hurt Hilda, she didn't want to hurt Brenda. I was just the one in the bloody middle. If I'd been a boy, it might have been different. It just got to the stage where I thought Mum hated me.

And still, I feel like I've painted Mum into a bad picture. *But* if I listen to what she said, I've got to put it in, because she didn't know what she was doing at the time, she was severely depressed and more or less out of it.

***

Some days it was hard for me to go and look for work, and when grandma died, I was made to stay home to help Mum out again. That didn't go well, unsurprisingly, and so I ended up going into Sydney itself for employment.

I was fifteen when I landed a great job in a factory that made baby clothes. I was called a picker because all I did was to cut cotton threads from the back of garments and make it neat enough for sale. I

enjoyed it for about three months, when our landlady 'butted in', telling Mum that there was a job going at the David Jones' main factory in Redfern (inner Sydney) and I could make more money working there.

So good old Mum made me leave this job for the one with more money. The David Jones factory made exclusive clothing for their retail stores and I stayed there for approximately a year, learning how to use the industrial sewing machines, which I enjoyed. It taught me how to make my own clothes, which helped me a lot in life, especially after my children came along years later.

I used to go to the canteen there every day and buy a couple of liquorice sticks or straps, and when it came to my sixteenth birthday, they all clubbed together and bought me a huge packet of liquorice sticks and straps.

***

Sometimes I was able to get out for a while, and spend time with Clive. He once drove us back to Warragamba Dam, and because he enjoyed photography, he asked me to stand beside this wheel-shaped part of the power house there and pretend I was holding it up.

"Holding up" part of the power station there.

I recall a time when Clive drove us up to the Blue Mountains, too, and while we were there, we went for a nice bush walk and picnic. It was very pretty with a lot more bushland in the area back then and Clive, as always, had his camera. Again, because he loved taking photographs, he set it up on a tri-pod and sat beside me on a log, and he tried to tell a bit of a funny story with each photo.

The story was supposed to be something like, a) "Come and sit beside me, dear", then b) "But I'm shy! No, we're all alone, I can't do that!", and c) "Then I have to smack your bottom!". It would have been quite funny, but I couldn't let Mum know how we had behaved, for she would not have approved it!

I even wrote in my photo album, "Only fooling," so that if she, or anyone else for that matter, ever saw these photos, she'd be okay with them. Clive and I were very proper back then!

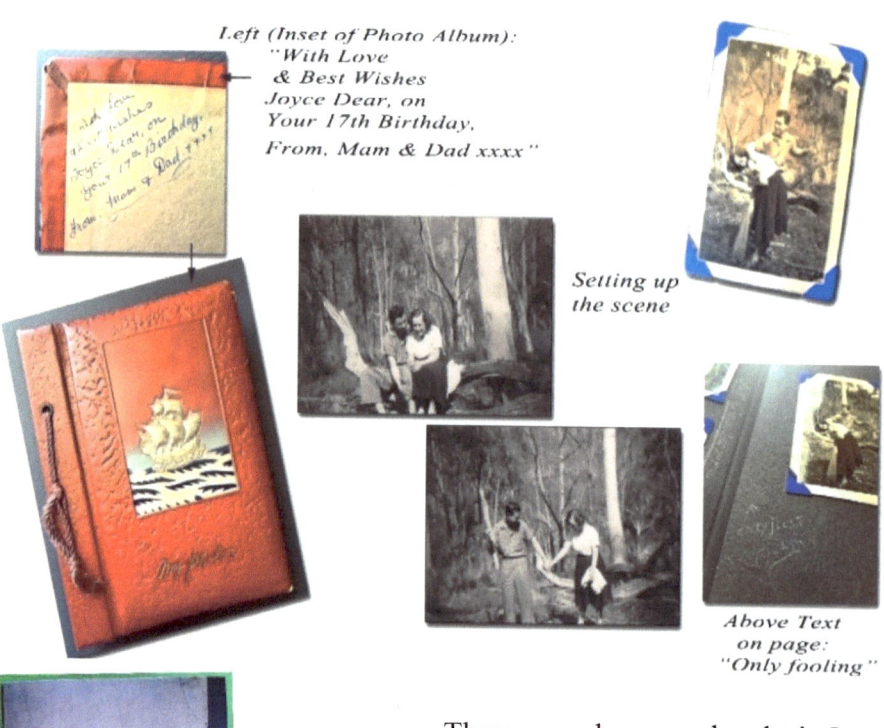

Left (Inset of Photo Album):
"With Love
& Best Wishes
Joyce Dear, on
Your 17th Birthday,
From, Mam & Dad xxxx"

Setting up
the scene

Above Text
on page:
"Only fooling"

By the back
of the house
at Ettalong

There was also a weekend trip I was allowed to go on with Clive and his Mum and Dad, to their holiday cottage up at Ettalong (on the Central Coast of N.S.W.). Clive took more photographs of me in my swimmers, (with their family dog) before we went to the beach.

ಌ

Dundas

Around early 1956 Mum told us we were moving again to a place called Dundas. She'd had her name on the housing commission list for a while and finally a house was available. So we were off again.

But this house was a beautiful mansion to anything we'd had before! And it was almost on the top of a slope, so we were looking out over the houses in our street. I remember when we'd first walked in the front door – there was this massive lounge room, with big windows that let lots of sunlight in.

Above: My sketch floor plan of our house in Dundas (in 1956; not to scale).

There was three good-sized bedrooms and a nice bathroom down a short hallway, and a kitchen and separate laundry towards the back of the house. The toilet was a great surprise – although it was still outside in the backyard, it was also a proper flushing toilet! Eventually Mum did get a second toilet put in the bathroom, but it would be a few years until that happened.

There was a bus stop just down around the corner from the house, and a small group of shops in the valley that took about ten-minutes to walk to. We could get to the train station or the main local shopping centre within about twenty minutes by bus or car. This place was far better than the last two homes and we loved it.

***

One afternoon while Clive and I were riding the train home, I felt a lot of pain in my tummy. It became so bad that I lay down on the carriage floor with my head just far enough out the door, and started throwing up. We got to Eastwood station where Clive's car was parked and he drove me straight to Top Ryde hospital, where we found out that I was suffering from an acute appendicitis.

He left me in the care of the staff as he had to go back to my place to tell Mum what had happened. He told me the next day that he'd had a hell of a time trying to convince her that I was in hospital; she didn't believe him and thought he was joking. He was frantic in trying to convince her and offered to take her to the hospital to see me. She actually went out to his car to look for me! Only for the fact that I wasn't there, she finally realised he was telling the truth!

She thought I was making it up and I was surprised that she hadn't come in straight away to tell me how ridiculous I was, as if I was looking for anything as an excuse to get out of work.

She did briefly come to see me about nine o'clock that night but only stayed for approximately ten minutes because the doctors said they had to operate on me straight away. They were told they could come back tomorrow, so we said goodnight, but I was glad to see the back of her!

When I was well enough, I went back to the David Jones factory, but left after two months because another job came up that was only a ten-minute walk from Central Station.

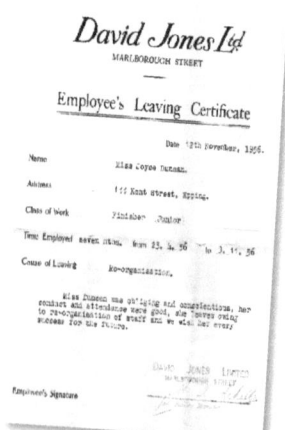

My leave certificate from David Jones.

***

Around sixteen-and-a-half, I started work in a swimwear factory in the suburb called Central, the heart of Sydney city. I was a factory hand, getting lunch orders, making teas and coffees for the workers and other general duties.

One day I needed to go from the second floor to the first floor. We didn't have lifts in this building, only stairs. I was on a long, narrow, spiral metal staircase when, like at Otford, it happened again. Halfway down I slipped. Not wanting to break my tailbone again, I put the palm of my right hand under my bottom, but the fall broke the bones in my hand.

I was sent home immediately, and from there, to hospital. The doctor took x-rays, which confirmed that my hand was broken in five places. I probably would have needed surgery, but by the time I could get an appointment at the hospital, it was too late for that. The doctors warned me that what they were going to do as a treatment would hurt – they just pulled my fingers very hard to straighten them, then wrapped them up in bandages. They weren't wrong, it did hurt!

But it meant I couldn't work for six weeks while they healed. So I was given a compensation payout from my employer, and eventually lost the job.

Me at 16 ½ after my broken hand accident, in a dress Mum made for me.

***

Me in my favourite dress bought from work.

When I was well enough to go back to work some six months later – now at around seventeen – I got a position as a machinist at *Pasadena* in Glebe, where I made skirts and blouses. I was so accustomed to handing over my wages to Mum that one day, on receiving my pay packet, I had an interesting conversation with a lady who worked with me.

I think I was wanting to buy a comic book and some food. Despite knowing that I couldn't just help myself to my own money, she was the one that convinced me to break into it for my own use. It's hard to recall this many years on, but I remember her being a bit of a tough girl, a bit on the plump side, and having nice blonde hair, and our conversation went something like this…

"I'm going shopping, do you want to come with me?" she asked.

"Oh I'd love to, but I don't have the money to buy anything," I remarked.

"You've got your pay packet there, why don't you break into it?" she asked.

"No, I'm not allowed to touch it," I said, a bit shyly.

"Why can't you? You've got the money there!"

"I have to give it all to my mum," I replied.

"Well surely to goodness you can take a little bit out?" she insisted. "Just tell your Mum that you needed the money!"

It wasn't that simple.

"No, if I do that Mum will kill me," I said, knowing the trouble I'd be in if I did.

"Don't give your mum *all* your pay packet!" she said. "If you want to buy something, buy something! She's got no right taking it off you!"

"But she's always taken it," I said. "I'm not allowed to touch it!"

"Keep *something* out of it," she persisted. "Just lie to her about having lost it or whatever."

I really wanted to do what she said. I wasn't sure if I could be game enough to do it, but eventually I ended up taking her advice – and nearly got killed for it.

I loved reading comics back then and when I saw a *Disney's Donald Duck* edition, I really wanted it.

'*Should I or shouldn't I,*' I asked myself.

I was shaking like a leaf when I reached in to my pay packet. It was only twenty pence, but I knew Mum would notice it missing.

'*What the heck!*' I thought, and bought it anyway. And it felt good buying it for myself! I knew I was going to get into trouble over it, but for once I was doing something for myself! Of course, Mum was very smart that way, nothing got past her. And by God did I get a yelling for it. I didn't get a belting, but I bloody-well got a verbal tirade.

When I arrived home that afternoon, the first thing I had to do, as usual, was hand her my pay packet – this time it was open.

She looked inside and with a scowl on her face, had it out with me.

"Okay, where's the rest of it?" she barked.

"Oh, I wanted to buy a comic," I stammered.

"*Why did you break into it?!*" she demanded. "You know you're supposed to bring the whole packet home!"

"Sorry," I murmured, and started to walk off to my room to change.

"You have no right to take that!" Mum yelled angrily, following behind. "That's mine!" That was her attitude. "You do *not* break into your pay packet! You ask me and *I'll* give it to you!"

It didn't matter what I said, she wouldn't listen.

"You do this again and look out!"

So I was very careful not to break into my pay packet again, until I got talking with that lady again.

"I got into so much trouble for spending my money on myself," I said.

"Look, the next time you get a pay rise or a bonus, don't tell her," she said. "Just keep giving her the same amount as you used to get and keep the rest for yourself. You've got to give yourself some freedom."

Well, I did. Somehow I managed to save a little money over time that she didn't know about.

Unfortunately I didn't get to keep my job at *Pasadena* though. Because my hand had been broken in so many places from the fall on the spiral stairs, it hurt to use it after only a few hours, and I couldn't steer the material under the needle quickly enough to get a good number of clothes made per hour. The boss came up to me one day and said that I wasn't getting my quoter out. They would have to let me go as I was too slow on the machine.

Left: Clive and I having fun in a photobooth at Town Hall train station. This photo-strip was lost in an old box of forgotten treasures!

Changing Jobs

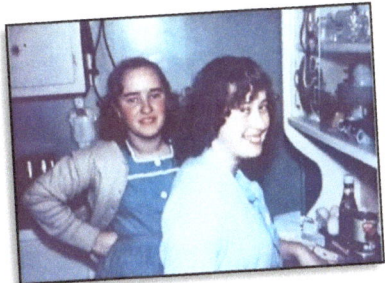

Clive snapping a candid picture of Brenda and I in the kitchen at Dundas.

I was about eighteen when Clive said, "Would you like to get married?"

Of course I would. It wasn't a formal proposal though, as we already knew between us that we were going to stay together for the rest of our lives. So the question itself went more or less unspoken, for it would be just a matter of time as to when we would get married. I'm sure he also felt sorry for me with Mum's attitude the way that it was. But it was nice to have it become an official thing that we were going to get engaged.

The ring would come eventually, as I was now changing jobs again. At around eighteen-and-a-half I started work in a factory at *Sargood Gardener* at Town Hall. It was much nearer to Central Station, and travel was easier than it was with the other jobs, as I had no need for busses or trams to take me the extra distance. An added bonus was that I would meet up with Clive after finishing for the day, as he worked in an office as a technician in the city, and we'd both take the same train together when going home. I was making men's hats, ties and handkerchiefs here, and was doing alright with it until, around six months on, my throat began to swell.

We had a metal container that we used to put our work in. It had a rigid, upright, square-shaped metal handle about an inch in diameter for carrying, and if only it had been rounded, or movable, I could have been alright.

As it was, one day I bent down to pick up some hats that were stacked beside it, but I accidentally over-reached and hit my throat on the square edge of the handle. It hurt and within a couple of days, my throat began to feel bad. It wasn't until a week later that I noticed it had swollen.

'What the hell's going on here?' I wondered.

I didn't understand what was happening at first, I just noticed that my neck was getting bigger over the following days, like a large tennis ball at first, and I was feeling like I was starting to choke. It was as if something inside was blocking my air-ways. Even Clive was concerned.

"Are you alright?" he asked one afternoon after work. "You don't look too good. Your throat's swelling up!"

"Yeah," I replied, "I don't know what's wrong. I hit my throat the other day on the metal handle."

"You should go and see the doctor about it," he said. "It's swelling right up!"

When I went to see a doctor, he was also concerned.

"You better go see a specialist," he said. "I think you've got something which looks very much like a goitre."

The specialist confirmed it was a goitre, and sent me to see Dr. Hale at Royal North Shore Hospital within the week.

On the day I was due to go to the hospital to see the doctor about it, I must have been in Mum's bad books. I'd had an afternoon appointment with the doctor at Royal North Shore Hospital, and I had planned on going to work for most of the day up until then. I remember talking with her about it the night before, but she wouldn't listen to me and told me that I wasn't allowed to go.

"Well I've got to go to work-" I started to say, but she cut me off.

"You're not going," she said, and in a nasty way, added, "You're staying home! If you have to go, *I'll* take you, and that's final!"

"Well Clive's going to pick me up in the morning on his way to work, and he'll take me down," I began.

"No," she insisted, "I said you're not going. As far as I'm concerned, if you have to go, I'll take you, but you're not going *anywhere* tomorrow! You're staying home!"

"Okay," I said reluctantly, wishing there was a way to get around this.

Later that evening Clive came to visit me and I managed to talk to him about it in private, and we decided to trick her...

"Well I'll come up in the morning," he said, "and pretend I'm coming to pick you up, and while your mum is telling me off, you sneak out the back door and get in the car and curl up on the floor in the front seat. I'll let you know when it's clear."

So the next morning he came to pick me up at the usual time for taking me to the station – about seven o'clock. He pulled up alongside of the house where Mum couldn't see the car, then he went around to the front door and spoke to her, knowing it was fruitless. I could hear her saying, "No I'm sorry, she's not going today. She's staying home!"

"Well, she's got to go to the hospital, she's got an appointment-"

"No, it doesn't matter, she doesn't need it. And she's not going to work today either!" she insisted. "If need be, *I'll* take her, but you're not taking her out of this house! She's staying home!"

Mum probably did have plans to take me to the appointment herself by bus, but her stubbornness was not letting on. Likely she thought I was still in my bedroom while she was busy bossing him around, but as far as I was concerned, I was still going to work that day!

So in the meantime, while she was distracted with him, I crept out the back door and jumped into the front seat of Clive's car. I closed the door as quietly as I possibly could, and folded myself down into a tight ball on the floor of the front seat, just as he'd instructed me to. The next minute he got in the car too.

"Okay, keep your head down," he murmured.

I wasn't game to lift it!

He started the engine and began reversing down the driveway.

"Yes and Mum's standing at the door waving to me," he said, and waved back to her. As we were going down the street and went out of sight, he gave me the all clear.

"You can come up now, it's safe," he said.

Only then I climbed up onto the seat, shaking like a leaf, terrified she was going to follow me somehow!

I told the boss at Sargood's about my appointment at work that day.

"I've got an appointment at the Royal North Shore hospital today, about two o'clock. I've got to go in about this sore throat."

He looked at me as if to say in a groaning sort of way, *'Oh, God!'*
But he didn't make a fuss.

"Oh, okay," he said, and let me go.

There wasn't much he could do about it and I was allowed to leave at around twelve-thirty to make my way to the appointment. I caught a train to St. Leonards Station, which was just down the road from the hospital, then took a short walk from there to the main entrance. After introducing myself to the lady in the office of the waiting room, I was told to sit down and the doctor would see me soon.

'*Come on Dr. Hale. Come on Dr. Hale,*' I kept thinking anxiously.

Within about ten to fifteen minutes, while I sat there waiting, I happened to see this figure walking briskly up the pathway to the front door with a scowl of utter rage on her face, looking like a wounded bull. I knew instantly it was my mum. And she was ready to kill me!

I panicked, so convinced that if she found me, she was going to yell, "You little bugger!" and whack me one – she would have done that there in the hospital in front of people. I know she would have because that was her nature. I was so sure that she probably would've attempted to kill me then and there, and despite the police being called in if she had, she'd still have screamed, "It's her bloody fault!"

So of course, I bolted, not stopping to tell anybody where I was going. I didn't care where I went so long as I could get well away from her as quickly as possible! I practically ran down the corridor in the opposite direction, where there was another corridor, found a back door open and went through that to the outside. I took off up a path in open space to a building on the top of a hill, which I think was a library, because there were books in there, or maybe it was a medical room, I didn't know; I was just too scared to care. And I hid in there, crying, terrified she would find me.

While I was standing at the window, just waiting to see her storming after me, a lady must have heard me and she came up to see how I was.

"Are you alright, Love," she asked. "What's the matter?"

"No, my Mum's down there and she's gonna kill me!" I replied.

"She won't kill you," the lady said.

'Yes she will!" I insisted. "I'm supposed to see Dr. Hale at two o'clock, but I can't see him because Mum's down there waiting for me, and if she sees me, she's gonna kill me because I left home!" I couldn't contain myself and blubbered away. "I ran away this morning and I wasn't supposed to- she didn't want me to come out-"

"Oh no, she won't kill you," she said. "Just stay there and I'll ring through to him."

I waited anxiously while she rang him, telling his assistant what was happening and could she please come up to get me. He sent his nurse, who couldn't have been much older than me, and I was still in hysterics when she arrived.

"Come on, Love," she said, "we're going to see Dr. Hale."

"*I can't* go down," I insisted, hesitating by the door. "Mum's in there!"

"It's alright, Love," she soothed. "You come with me. We're going in the back way-"

"But if she sees me, she'll kill me!"

"No she won't," she said. "We'll take you down to see Dr. Hale. Mum's sitting in another room. We've got her out of the way for you."

That calmed me a little bit. She somehow convinced me it was safe enough to go back and she held my hand all the way, taking me to his little office.

"When we're ready for her, we'll bring your mum in," she said.

"Don't do that!" I cried, "because she's going to kill me!"

"No she won't," she said assuredly. "She won't do nothing while we're here."

I was so scared, not believing a word of it.

Finally the doctor came in to see me.

"Please take a seat," he said. "Now, what is the problem?"

I told him everything in a rush. "And because of this nonsense," I said on finishing, "she won't let me come into hospital to have the operation."

He asked me a few questions, which I answered correctly, checking my eyes, pulse and throat as he did. "My you've got the nerves bad," he commented with concern. "Put your hands straight out in front of you."

I did as he asked, but they started to shake.

"Can you steady your hands a bit more?"

He put a sheet of paper on them.

It almost fell off them because they were shaking so badly. I couldn't keep them still.

"My God," he said, "you've got a bad case of the nerves! This is the worst case I've seen in anybody – in many, many years." He took the sheet away, and looked at me sternly. "I can tell you now, you're not going home. You can't. You're going into hospital. We'll put you in now! We're going to have to get you settled for two weeks just to calm your nerves down."

"What about Mum?" I started, "She's gonna kill me if you tell her that!"

"It doesn't matter," he said. "She's going to be coming in here anyhow. In fact, we'll get your mum in now and I'm going to sit and talk to her in front of you, and you're not going to move; you're going to sit right there and I'm going to put her there, opposite you," he said, pointing to an extra chair. "I'll explain it all to her. And the nurse will keep an eye on her for you."

My eyes flew wide open. *What?! Now?! In here?!*

"She won't start anything," he said. "We won't let her."

So Mum came in shortly after – I could hear her heels going *clip-clop* on the floor. I didn't want to look at her, but did anyway. She gave me a foul scowl and kept up this hard stare while Dr. Hale asked her some questions.

"I'm taking my daughter home with me," she then told him.

"No, Joyce is not going home today," he began. "In fact, I'm sorry to tell you Mrs. Duncan, but your daughter is very, very sick and we're putting her into hospital right *now*. She's being admitted in, so I want you to go back to the waiting room desk and fill in all the paper work."

She must have given a horrified look of protest, because he added, "We don't need your permission. She's very, very stressed out! And I don't want you to have any contact with Joyce for at least a week. We'll estimate when you can come and see her. Her nerves are shot to pieces!"

She turned to me with a strange glare, as if to say, '*You're putting it all on, I know you are! You little bugger!*'

"She's in such a desperate state that she could collapse at any moment," he added severely. We can't have her upset any more than she already is. We'll let you know when you can come and visit her."

Then Mum was escorted out of his room, and soon the nurse returned and took me down to the ward where I was going to be kept. I never saw Mum for at least a week after that because they wouldn't allow her near me.

That night Clive came to visit me.

"They told me they'd admitted you in," he said, taking my hand. "And if I want to come and visit you, I can, but they also said *don't* bring the mother!"

It was such a relief to hear how strict they were being about it.

Clive at work, setting up a planetary camera to photograph some engineering drawings.

"And they said that they'll let her know when she can visit, but it won't be unless there is a staff member with her to keep an eye on her."

He visited me every night after work, and even his own mum and dad came once.

***

At the end of that first week, apparently Mum was allowed to come in for about fifteen minutes.

"But if your mum upsets you at any stage," they said, "a nurse will be standing by for you, watching to see how you are. If you feel upset, tell her and she will escort your mother out again."

Dad was so happy to see me, though sorry to see where I was. Mum still had a bit of a grudge and I could see she wanted to go mad on me –

but she wasn't allowed to. It must have been very hard for her to keep her cool, because after what turned out to be about half an hour, she decided they needed to leave.

"Oh well," she said with tight lips, "we'd better go home now."

They left, while Clive stayed with me.

***

Two weeks after being admitted in, right on Christmas, my nerves had settled enough and I had the operation. They cut my throat from one side right across to the other, and I had to have about thirty stitches to close it back up. It looked like somebody had slashed my neck! I couldn't lift my head up properly as it was sort of stuck down for the skin to reseal.

One of my favourite Christmas cards.

So at eighteen, I spent New Year's eve in hospital. The nurses came around at nine o'clock and gave us sleeping tablets, so that we'd all be asleep while they could go off and enjoy the fireworks. I didn't want to take it, but they stood over me, watching, and then asking me to open my mouth afterwards to see that it had been swallowed. I missed out on the celebrations – but at least I also missed out on Mum's temper!

༄༅

News 1959: Three of the most famous American singers die in a plane crash.

Recovery

It took quite a while for my neck to heal and I was in there for about four weeks overall. Every morning the doctor would say, "Come on, you can lift your head up a bit more than it is."

So I had to try and force my head to lift up. After about three or four days of this, he must have thought I was getting better.

One of my get-well cards.

"Okay," he said one morning, "we'll let your mum come back now, and just see how she reacts with you. *If* she is okay, we'll let you go home soon, but not just yet. We'll give you to the end of the week, first."

Mum was on her best behaviour.

"If all goes well," the doctor said to her, "we'll let Joyce come home at the end of the week, and we can't have you upsetting her, otherwise she'll end up back in hospital."

I think it must've been very, very hard for her to keep her cool. I can still see her face today whenever I think about this time in my life. I'd say both my dad and sister must have coaxed her every time she looked like she was going to get cranky.

"Calm down. Calm down," they would have said. "You can't get Joyce upset!"

And I can almost hear her response.

"I'm not trying to upset her! She's a bloody fool!"

It was a situation where you couldn't predict whether she was going to fly off the handle or not. It was touch and go there for a while and if she'd have played up just once and upset me in the hospital, I honestly think the doctor would have stepped in with, "No, Joyce is going to a foster home!" Or maybe they would have put me into a different home altogether, perhaps asking Clive to help them find me another place to live so I could avoid the constant abuse.

But thankfully Mum did restrain herself and eventually I was sent home. She was on her best behaviour for at least two weeks, and at about the third week, I was well enough to go back to work.

When I returned to Sargood's, I just wasn't fast enough for them, plus I was sick of sewing, so after a month I left this job to do a different kind of work. I went down the road from them the next day and found a job with John Sands, which was a big, well-known company that made boxes and all types of cards, but were probably best known for making board games, such as *Monopoly*, *Cluedo*, *Scrabble* and *The Game of Life*, to name a few. I asked the boss if I could work there.

"What sort of work are you used too?" he asked.

"I've been on sewing machines all my years, and I'm sick of them," I answered.

"Well, are you sure that you're going to get used to our machines? They're not sewing machines."

"No that's alright!" I eagerly said, "I don't mind!"

So I went in and he showed me what I had to do. I was given the task of folding the lids of the boardgame boxes; I was taught to fold first one side, then the next side, then the other side and then the fourth side. Each box type had to be done in a certain manner, and we had to do quite a lot in a quota.

For the first two or three days I was carefully doing one at a time, and I was watching the other people there who had more experience – they were piling their folded boxes up: I was maybe getting ten done to their twenty. So I paid closer attention to how they were folding them.

Where I was being so careful to fold one box lid at a time, they had a pile of about half a dozen boxes, turning them all over together, squashing the sides down, and putting them aside. They were doubling more that way than what I was doing. By the time I got say, ten lids done, they had nearly fifty or sixty done. No wonder they were getting their quota!

So I tried the same thing, at first stacking two or three lids together, folding them in unison, then adding a couple more, until I could manage several at the same time. I was soon getting the folded pile up, and the boss was impressed the way I was getting my quota filled – I learnt very quickly!

Then I was put in another room on the other side of the factory, where they were putting bookbinding strips on the edges of the boardgames. They showed me how to use this machine; I would put in this black type of tape in one side and cut it off at the other end. Oh I loved that machine!

Then I got walked around to see how the printers worked. This is where I met John Hunt, a man whose family went on to become good friends with us for many years. John's machine printed off all the paper parts of a game. The big sheet that rolled off it looked just like a newspaper ream as pictures and words rolled out onto a conveyor belt.

From there, the printed sheets were taken to another machine in the corner of the factory, where two girls worked with another conveyor belt. At one part of it, the printed paper came out of a machine with a gooey, sticky film on the back of it. At the other end, the original, plain box lid that I'd folded earlier, was laid out for the sheet to be stuck to it.

I wasn't sure exactly what I was doing, and I missed a couple of them because I'd had them on a slight angle, but I persevered. I had to put the box down on the sticky paper, which was on a continually moving belt. Then the girl would take that box and fit the sheet into the corners, and re-fold the sides. Then suddenly there was the picture of the game on the lid of the box! Oh I enjoyed that machine very much!

I loved working there and I was able to buy new games that came out on the market at factory prices! I lasted there for about two years, not for being too slow, but because of something better…

Some of the games I bought from John Sands

***

Sometime in my nineteenth year, Clive and I finally went to a jeweller for my engagement ring. Our relationship with Mum was still rather rocky, but we defied her anyway. Back when I was in hospital

Memories From My Past

with the goitre, he told me of the conversation they'd had about our desire to get married.

He'd been driving her back home from seeing me at Royal North Shore and they were around the Carlingford area on the way to Dundas when he raised the topic.

"I want to marry Joyce," he'd said.

Surprisingly she was alright about it!

"Okay," she'd said.

So with nearly five years of being together, there we were, ready to take the next step.

There was an arcade in the city where Clive worked, with a jewellery shop right at the bottom, called *Freeman's*. I told the man what I liked and he showed us a few rings, with one having little stones in the corners and its band was both silver and gold. I liked the combination of the two colours; I didn't want an all-silver or all-gold ring.

"Oh that's beautiful, isn't it?" I said.

"Would you like it?" Clive asked.

"Oh yes," I said, smiling.

The man then put a multiple ring sizer on my finger to check what size number I needed. The pretty ring fit, and Clive bought it. Mum nearly fainted when she found out! However finally, we were now officially engaged.

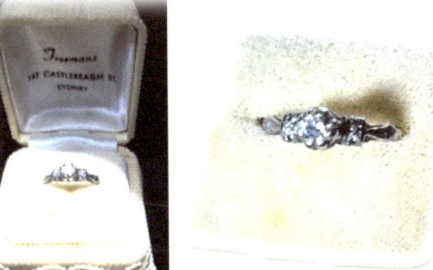

Right: Clive's engagement ring for me, in its original box.

The building of the Warragamba Dam took about twelve years and in 1960, Dad received an invitation to its official opening. The whole family was included, and we dressed in our best for the festive event. It was so good to see the old area again, seeing how it had slowly changed over the years.

Above: *"The group again, ready to go to a ball at Warragamba".*
From Left: Me, Clive, Brenda, Dad, Mum, and Hilda, with Allan behind the camera.

Left: *The invitation to attend the official opening of the dam, Friday 14th October 1960.*

The Griffith Holiday

At twenty I was still not getting on with Mum, (even after I'd left hospital we hadn't got along). Almost a year had gone by and the Christmas holidays following my 20th birthday had come. My family, Clive and I went on a camping trip to Griffith, down on the south coast of NSW. My sister, Hilda, was now engaged to Allan, and he and his parents, Mr. and Mrs. Janes, and one of their daughters, Lynette, also came along with us.

Dad couldn't find an available caravan park for us as all the camping grounds were full. It looked like we'd have to set up camp in a paddock somewhere. Dad drove back into town and stopped in at the local post office. He met a man in there and they got talking, when Dad said something about the accommodation problem.

"It's because it's Christmastime," the man said. "How about you come back to my place? I've got a big paddock out the back door, you can put your tent up in there!"

Dad was over the moon and we followed him back to his farm. It was a nice big yard and we set up our tent beside his tin shed. We were there about a week when trouble erupted.

Being summer, it was a very hot, stinking day. It was so damned hot, we couldn't breathe. Every time we opened our mouth we were breathing in hot air. You couldn't do anything about it; you just had to put up with it, and we'd just finished lunch. Mum had started to wash up the dishes in a large tub, and Mrs. Janes, Hilda's mother-in-law-to-be, began to help her with drying them. But Mum wasn't too happy about it.

"Are you going to give us a hand?" she said in a cranky way.

"Yeah okay," I replied, getting up and grabbing a tea towel.

I started wiping the cloth over things very slowly, because the heat was unbearable. Mum glanced at me – and she saw fire.

She started again – in front of Mrs. Janes!

"Hurry up! Can't you go any faster than that?" she cried.

"Oh it's hot!" I said, feeling like I was literally melting.

"I don't care what it is!" she snapped. "You're too slow!"

I tried moving faster, but it wasn't good enough. She was already too cranky with me.

"Look here! You're taking too long!" she retorted, and suddenly lashed out. She grabbed me by the front of my top, her hand in a tight fist, and she dragged me over to the shed, where she bailed me up against the hot tin and started hitting me, slapping me around the face and banging my head against the wall.

"And don't you back-answer me!" she railed.

I couldn't help crying, which probably made her crankier. This was happening *in front* of Mr. and Mrs. Janes, Hilda's in-laws to be, and everyone else who was around me at the time. I can still see the look of shock on Mrs. Jane's face. It was my last straw.

"Look I'm very sorry," Mrs. Janes said after Mum stepped back, "but Bill and I have to go home tomorrow. We can't stay."

"Oh?" Mum said in the uncomfortable silence.

"Yes, Lynette's not feeling very well," she remarked. "She will be better back in her own home."

In that moment, I made my mind up to go with them.

"Can I come home with you," I asked.

"Yes, if you want, Dear," she said.

"You're not going!" Mum called out. "You can stay here!"

"Well I'm not staying here any longer!" I cried back. "I've had enough! I'm going home with Mr. and Mrs. Janes!"

The next day Mrs. Janes let me go home with them, because they now knew my situation with Mum.

As Clive and I got in the car, Mum had to have the last word.

"And don't you be home when I get back!" she yelled angrily. "Make sure there's nothing there!"

Well, that was my cue to get out of the house. *'Right, okay,'* I thought, *'I'll do exactly what you want!'*

We were late getting back to my house, so I stayed there for the night on my own, as Clive left with the others to go back to his parent's place. I felt free at last! No more arguments! I had a good night's sleep, as I had made up my mind to go looking for a place to rent the very next day.

Clive came back in the morning to pick me up, bag and all. I had grabbed what I could of my things and then we went house-hunting. He drove me around to a few places but unfortunately everything was too expensive.

I looked in the local papers under "Rentals" and found one in Harris Park, which was a very bad area then, but I

didn't know that and the unit was cheap enough for me and my options weren't great. Clive took me to see Mrs. Janes so I could let her know where I was going. When I mentioned the location, she was horrified.

"In case you're interested, Clive's going to take me over to Harris Park, we're going to go look at a place that's for rent there."

"Oh no! Please don't go there!" she begged.

"Why?" I asked, not knowing anything about the area.

"Do you know how violent it is? It's a very bad area!"

"But I can't afford to go anywhere else!" I replied.

"There are a lot of hoodlums there, thieves and murderers and things. There's a lot of vandalism in that place too! You could get attacked and you can get killed there too! No, you can't go there!" she insisted.

"I don't have a choice!" I said, wishing it wasn't true.

"Please, if you're going to go there, I'd rather you came here. You'll be much safer."

She got up and went to have a talk to her husband, and when she came back, she said, "Bill said you can stay here,"

I could hardly say no. So I went back to Mum and Dad's house to pack the rest of my things and returned back to their house before dinner, very relieved to have a safe roof over my head.

I was told that when Mum had arrived home a few days later to find that I really had moved out, she was furious. But I didn't care. This lovely, caring lady took me in, knowing now how Mum had treated me so badly.

Mum never spoke to me for eight months.

***

Mr. and Mrs. Janes had had four children; two boys and two girls. The sisters, Beverly and Lynette, shared the main big bedroom in the front of the house. Beverly was about seventeen, going on eighteen when I moved in, and Lynette was about fourteen. Their mum fitted another single bed in there for me – right in the middle between their beds, which didn't go down well with Beverly.

Mrs. Janes (when she was in her 70's).

She took an instant dislike to me. She was Mrs. Janes' pet, her first-born daughter, and it was quite possibly because I was older than her that she felt so angry towards me. I don't know, but having my bed where it was would have been an insult to her, I suppose. It must have felt cramped to her too, now that I was sharing her space, for they had been used to just the two of them.

Every day was the same with her, no matter how I behaved towards her. Whenever I said "Hi," or asked how she was, her response was blunt.

"Good," she might quip as she'd instantly turned away from me. Or if she was quick enough, she would have turned around and left before I could say anything.

She was always cold to me, whether we were alone or had company around, and she tended to avoid me wherever possible. And I avoided her for the most part, somehow putting up with her, because being here was better than living in a dangerous neighbourhood. I stayed with this family for just on twelve months.

In a way, her behaviour was worse than Mum's as she ignored me completely! Yet there were many times where things had happened that I *knew* she'd been behind it, lots of little things that were moved, went missing or were misplaced, that made me look bad or were simply to frustrate me. For example, I might have put my cup down on the bench by the kettle, say, and I'd walk away to get something, and when I came back, my cup would be on the table.

There was a night I was lying in bed and I felt this furry thing move across my face. I brushed my hand there and heard *thump* on the floor. I put the torch on to see what it was – and a rat ran off into the dark!

I don't know if it came in by itself, or if she'd put it on my pillow, but I can well imagine that with her attitude the way it was, she'd either put it on my pillow or somewhere on the bed. That was like her way of saying to me, "Get out of here. I don't want you in here!"

I just ignored it, I had to. In a way I felt sorry for her that she could be so petty.

My sister's wedding,
(from left) Me, Beverly, Hilda, Sheila and Brenda.

***

Memories From My Past

I really loved working at John Sands and kept on with them over the rest of that year. I was so used to handing over my whole pay to Mum that at the end of that week, I went to offer Mrs. Janes my pay packet, but she refused and gave it back to me.

"Thank you very much, there's my pay packet," I had said.

"Sorry Darling, I don't want it," she replied, smiling.

"Well you've got to have something for me staying here!" I insisted.

"Well if you want to give me something, just give me ten pound towards the food!" she said. It came as quite a surprise.

"Are you sure?" I asked.

"Yes, Dear. That should be enough to put towards the shopping."

'*Wow!*' I thought, '*what a change from Mum!*'

I was a bit stunned, but she knew my mum, I guess, and so she must have been happy to let me keep much of my money.

So it was Mrs. Janes who introduced me to what paying board was, and I was thrilled to be able to give her that ten pounds and *still* keep the rest of my pay packet!

*Three of my pay-slips
found in a worn-out box of
old treasures!*

My Twenty-First Birthday

I stayed with the Janes' family until just after I had turned twenty-one, as Clive and I had decided to get married on the first weekend in December.

I remember the night of my twenty-first birthday because it was full of surprises. Clive was supposed to be taking me to his brother's place at Caringbah, where we were going to have a party starting at seven

One of my 21st Birthday cards.

o'clock. It was a good forty-five minutes' drive away, yet it was coming up for six-thirty and we were still at Mrs. Jane's house! I was getting myself all worked up with fear that we were running late, as Clive kept hesitating, saying things like he wouldn't be much longer, or that he'd be ready soon.

"Bob won't be too happy if we're late at their place," I said to him.

"It's alright," Clive soothed. "He knows that I'm going to be late."

He was hanging back for some reason and I couldn't understand why he seemed to be stalling. I had no idea that they were all cooking something up for me. By six-forty-five there was a knock on the front door of the house.

"Go and open it," he said, "because there might be a surprise for you."

When I opened the door, who should be standing there?

Mum and Dad!

I nearly died.

She had a scowling look on her face.

"Just came to give you a birthday present. That's all," she said, tight-lipped.

"Oh… do you want to come in?" I nervously asked. "Because you can have a cup of tea-"

"No, we can't stop," she interrupted, almost grudgingly handing me the gift.

"Oh, well, thank you very much for the present," I began nervously, reaching forward to hug Dad. I wanted so much to give him a long, loving cuddle, and to show him my appreciation for turning up this night. But all I got in return was a cold hug, more of a pat around the shoulders that I'm sure was only to acknowledge me and avoid an argument about it from Mum. I felt nervous as we hadn't spoken to each other in months, then I thought I had better say something about our upcoming wedding. It should have been exciting news, but all I felt was intimidation.

"Clive and I are getting married on December the second, and I would like Dad to give me away," I said timidly.

Dad's eyes lit up with a smile. He was about to reply when Mum tugged at his arm and jumped in with, "No. He can't! He's not going to give you away!"

Dad looked devastated.

"And we're going home!" she snapped, turning to bustle Dad off with her. Then she added in a very, *very* nasty way, "And we're *not* going to come to your wedding!"

I could see the anger in her face! And I can still see that steely gaze today. She more or less forced Dad back to the car with her, walking stiffly and looking hard as she sat in the front seat. Dad looked miserable. I'm sure my father wanted to stay, and I'm quite positive he'd love to have accepted my request to our wedding.

But Mum was the boss. It seemed she'd always been so. I guess Dad was never game enough to stand up to her. He was a gentle, quiet man who just went along with things. I wonder now if he didn't have the confidence to tell her to stay out of things when it really mattered.

I sadly watched them drive away. Because of her rotten attitude, I felt awful, and it left a bad taste in my throat. I wanted to throw up. It was a horrible, traumatic experience that I never want to see happen again.

I went back into the kitchen where Clive and Mr. and Mrs. Janes were now standing around. I told them what Mum had said.

"Well, that's alright, don't worry about it," Clive said, trying to console me. "We'll work around it."

About ten minutes later there was another knock at the front door.

'Oh beaut! Mum's come back to apologise!' I thought, hurrying for the door. *'Hopefully she's changed her mind!'*

I opened the door with anticipation, but I was disappointed.

Clive's brother, Bob, and his wife, Dot, had arrived.

"What are you doing here?" I asked, a bit shocked and suddenly remembering that we were supposed to be going to their place. "We're running late!"

"Yes, I know," Dot said, smiling.

Clive had quietly stepped in beside me and gently said, "Surprise."

We hugged our visitors and I took their present for me.

"We were going to go to their place," he continued, "but they suggested coming up here to have a party with Mr. and Mrs. Janes, because they've been so kind to us, taking you in, putting a roof over your head and doing what they can for you. Then Hilda and Allan organised the rest with them."

My older sister and her fiancé also arrived soon after them, and we had a lovely little get together.

Clive and I on my twenty-first birthday.

ಐಜ

Memories From My Past

A
New
Family

Getting Married

Following my birthday, I began to make arrangements to marry my beautiful fiancé. I had three months to sort everything out before 2nd December. Thanks to Mrs. Janes allowing me to keep most of my wages, I was able to save a little bit each week and put my wedding dress on lay-by. I'd go and put half of my money onto paying it off, as well as the other little things that I wanted for the day – and the best part was that I didn't have to worry about Mum going mad on me. I was so grateful for this wonderful lady being in my life!

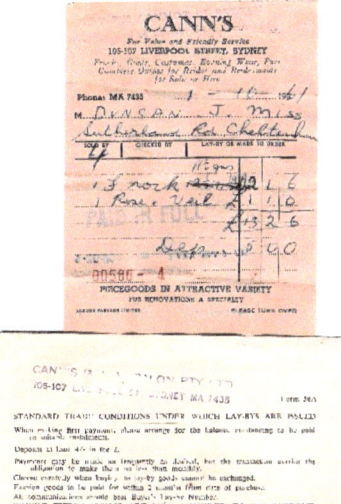

Part of my bridal lay-by, somehow kept all of these years, found in a worn out box of old treasures!

Clive and I were paying for our own special day, so I had to limit myself as to who I could have. I asked Clive's sister-in-law, Jean, to be my maid of honour, and one of my girlfriends that I worked with to be my bridesmaid. There was a little girl, called Kim, that lived opposite Mum and Dad in Dundas, who I rather liked. I thought she was a beautiful kid, and I asked her mother if I could have her for my flower girl.

The ladies' dresses had a taffeta petticoat with a pretty nylon cover of the same colour, which had floral print on it and was scalloped at the knee on the hem. Jean was in a soft pink dress, my girlfriend, Beverly, was in a pale blue one, and I let the flower girl's mum come up with a dress to match those colours. It turned out like a lovely lavender, as she'd made the petticoat in blue taffeta and the covering layer in pink floral-printed nylon. The ladies' headpieces were a large flower with spreading net (that matched their dress), and Kim's headpiece was two

My bridesmaids, flower girl, and I on my wedding day.
(from left) Beverly Bayliss, me, Kim and Jean.

floral half-circlets, worn as a connecting circle. I had a tiara.

My older sister, Hilda, had married Allan a week before our wedding. I was one of her bridesmaids (*see page 145 for picture*). Hilda was Mum's favourite, she was her pet and she couldn't do anything wrong, so Mum had to go to their wedding – well, she didn't *have* to go, of course, but she clearly was happy to. She got all nicely dressed up for the occasion – and never said "boo" to me all day. It was like I wasn't there. Hilda may have even said to her not to start any arguments at her wedding.

But I did get to talk with Dad, and I asked him if they would come to my own wedding. I could see he wanted to and he said that he would work on Mum so that he could at least walk me down the aisle. It felt promising, and I really hoped he would.

It was really bothering me that I might not have my father at my own wedding. From what I'd seen, every bride had their father give them away (or father-figure, someone they loved as a father). I wanted mine to be there with me – my dad; we had been so close in life.

I hadn't heard anything from them over the next couple of days, so I rang Mum, to see if she had changed her mind. It seemed nothing had changed though.

"No, I've already told you! He's not giving you away!" she snapped. "Don't expect us to come! That's it! That's final!" That was her answer, and she hung up on me.

What was I going to do? I needed *someone* to walk me down the aisle and I only had two days to go. I decided to ask the minister what I could do.

"Well if your dad can't give you away," he said, "would you like me to walk you down the aisle?"

"Oh that'd be lovely!" I said, smiling with relief. "Thank you very much."

Thankfully I would now have someone beside me to take me to my new husband.

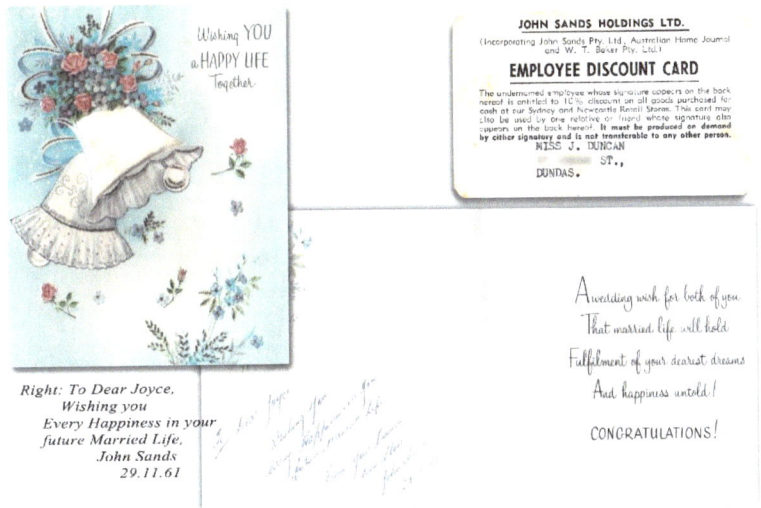

Right: To Dear Joyce,
Wishing you
Every Happiness in your
future Married Life,
John Sands
29.11.61

***

On the morning of my wedding, I woke up at about eight o'clock, feeling so happy and excited about the day to come. My wedding dress was hanging over the wardrobe mirror, fresh from the shop the afternoon before.

'*I'm going to be wearing that soon,*' I thought, looking at it. I got up and put my dressing gown on, all eager to get started.

I couldn't see any signs of Beverly in the bedroom or on my way to the kitchen to have my breakfast.

"Where's Beverly?" I asked Mrs. Janes when I met her there. "I can't see her. Is she here?" I thought she was coming to the wedding and might have been getting her cereal or something. Although she didn't like me, she never said she wasn't going to come to it.

"No," she said, "She's gone to the zoo with her boyfriend. She's not going to the wedding."

"Oh, what a shame," I replied, feeling sorry that she couldn't accept me. Lynette, her younger sister, was coming and we had always got on well together.

"I'm sorry about Beverly," I said to Mrs. Janes as we chatted through the meal.

"Oh, don't worry about her," she said. "She'll be alright."

After breakfast, I took a shower and returned to the room to put my underwear on, covering myself with my dressing gown again as I had almost three hours to fill before the car was due to arrive.

Every time I walked back into the room that morning, I looked at the dress and said, '*Going on soon!*' Like any bride, I was looking forward to wearing it.

Around twelve-forty, Mrs. Janes must have been wondering if I was taking my time.

"Are you going to get dressed?" she asked, smiling.

"I suppose I'd better," I said, "because the girls will be turning up soon."

I went into the bedroom, happy that it was finally time to put my beautiful dress on. It was made of tulle and lace and was full-length with a wide skirt, and I still have it today. But as I lifted it down from the top of the wardrobe, I had quite a rude shock – white cream had been smeared all over the mirror! Luckily there was a big, clear plastic bag protecting the dress, but the mirror was completely smeared in what I think was skin cream from Beverly's make-up. I know it was done so that I couldn't see myself.

"Aahh Mrs. Janes!" I called, feeling quite anxious.

She came in quickly.

"What's up?" she asked.

"Look at the mirror," I said, dismayed.

"Oh no," she cried with a frown. "Naughty Beverly! I'll have a talk to her when she comes home. Don't worry about it. I'll fix it up."

She went and got some warm, soapy water and cleaned the mirror down, as I carefully removed my dress from the bag and put it on. Beverley's act brought me a lot of sadness to think that she would do that to me, and I'd never done anything to her to give her reason for it. She was angry because, I feel, that I had muscled in on her territory, when she was her mum's favourite daughter.

The strange part to it is that Mrs. Janes was a Jehovah's Witness, and

Beverly was supposedly following in her footsteps! I imagine that her attitude was more along the lines of, '*you're trying to take my mother away from me!*' I was possibly wrong about this idea, yet she knew it was only going to be for a short while.

Well, she had to wear this, not me. As far as I was concerned, this was my day and I couldn't care less about her. It no longer mattered that she didn't want to come to my wedding!

***

The bridesmaids arrived and quickly put their dresses on, while Mr. and Mrs. Janes and Lynette left for the church. The flower girl came down, already dressed, and I thought she looked so pretty.

"Oh you're going to look beautiful at the wedding!" I said to her, so pleased I'd picked her for the role.

She smiled brightly.

I think her mum was proud, too.

At about one-thirty, we finished putting our headpieces in place and by around quarter to two, our bridal cars pulled up outside. So we picked up our bouquet and posies and went out.

I got in mine, feeling all so excited, thinking, '*Oh I'm going to get married!*'

It was about a five-minute walk from Mrs. Janes' house to church, and I could have walked there, but of course, what bride will do that when she's got transport? So the drivers decided to take us up and around the block to give the guests time to get into the church. Funnily enough, a girlfriend I had known from school had also chosen the same time and day to get married. As my car was going up the hill, I saw her in her bridal car coming down the opposite way. She was going to the Methodist Church in Epping as I was going to the Congregational

Church right on the corner. We just waved to each other as we passed in the street, laughing at the chance encounter.

And then we arrived at the church.

My excitement became nerves as we walked into the foyer. It was really happening. At long last I was going to marry the man I loved! The man my mother didn't like. And a thought of not seeing my dad beside me almost made me cry. We stood there waiting only a few minutes when the minister gently came up to me.

"Are you ready to go now?" he asked.

I still desperately wanted my dad to be there. It was *his* job, *his* daughter's wedding. I looked to the door as if I might see him walking in, smiling that wonderful smile and reaching out to take my arm. But it wasn't happening. The minister had his finger on the button, ready to ring through to the pianist, and I could hear that everyone inside had fallen quiet, just waiting for the music to start. I took a deep breath and nodded.

"Yes, I'm ready," I said.

I was literally just about to walk down the aisle, the Minister was just about to press the button, when Hilda raced into the foyer.

"Stop! Stop!" she quietly shouted.

We paused.

"Don't do anything just yet!" she whispered loudly.

"Why?" I asked, wondering what was so urgent.

"They're coming!"

"Who's coming?" I said.

"Mum and Dad! They're on their way right behind me!"

I caught my breath. Hilda must have worked a miracle on Mum, and my surprise must have shown on my face.

"Dad will give you away!" she cried.

I couldn't believe it, but sure enough, there they were coming in the door just a moment behind her. Somehow, between the two of them, they must have changed Mum's mind.

"Oh, thank goodness," I heard the minister say beside me. "Are you going to be alright?"

"Yes," I said, smiling too, "if Dad's come, he'll walk me down."

"Okay," he said, and left to go into the church.

I could hardly believe what I saw. Mum, surprisingly, was dressed in a pretty pink floral dress. I know she had some beautiful dresses, and I'm guessing this was one of the best in her wardrobe. She looked quite nice! But she must have still been cranky, because she didn't smile at me. She didn't even say something like, "Gee you look pretty" or, "gee you look nice".

She had that typical hard scowl on her face that was really saying, '*Huh, you won after all, didn't you? You might have won this round, but I am not happy!*' She stormed off into the church with Hilda and Allan.

But then there was Dad.

His face said it all. He looked just like a big kid who'd just won the lottery, dressed in his best suit and brimming from ear to ear. You could see how happy and proud he was, and it really made my day! He hurried to my side and took my left hand into his arm.

"Hi, you look beautiful," he said.

My heart swelled.

My Dad's lovely smile.

"Oh thanks, Dad," I said, tearing up.

His big, magnificent smile filled me with so much happiness and love, and I've never forgotten that adoring look.

The minister nodded to the pianist.

The music started.

We stepped forward. It was like a dream come true, I was walking down the aisle to marry my beautiful man, whom I loved very much, *and* I was being given away to him by my beloved father! I had *his* blessings at least, even if Mum didn't give me hers. So much for getting involved with an Australian! We had defied her all the way, and this was the icing on the cake.

I happened to see that Mum didn't even sit down at the front – she was about halfway down in the rows.

When we got down to the end of the aisle and saw Clive, he was beaming with happiness. Dad stood proudly at my side as the service began.

"Ladies and gentlemen," the minister started, and then soon he came to that special part, "Who should give this woman away?"

Dad stepped forward.

"I do," he said with a big smile, then he stepped back and went over to see Mum, where he whispered something to her. I suspect he might have warned her to keep quiet.

And there was no interruptions when the minister asked if anyone objected to this marriage. I'm surprised when I think back on it that Mum hadn't spoken up – maybe she knew she wasn't going to get away with it.

Mum barely spoke to me all day, even at the reception. But I didn't care. Dad was with me and that was all that mattered. I'm thankful to Hilda for talking Mum into it. After all, she *was* Mum's favourite daughter!

***

After the wedding, everyone did comment on how lovely we looked and, as I had thought, on how beautiful the flower girl was. Looking back, I wished we'd had a professional photographer. Instead, we got a friend of my brothers to take our photos.

His name was Tommy Macintyre, but we all called him Hop-along, because he had one leg shorter than the other, and this gave him a wobble when he walked.

Clive worked with Rank Xerox at that stage, and he could buy rolls of film much cheaper through his work. He also had the means to develop film in the backyard shed of his parent's place. So as we were needing to keep the costs down, it was a practical thing to get someone we knew to take pictures for us.

"If I give you a camera, will you take some photos for us?" he asked Hop-along in the weeks leading up to the day. "I have some film through work, and I'll have them developed *my* way by doing this."

"Yes, Mate!" he said. "I can do that!"

"Good. Just take some photos as best as you can."

Clive gave him three rolls of film, but he only used about two-and-a-half on the day, taking photos seemingly at random. He took one of us when we got to the church, one of us getting out of the cars, another one inside the church, and another one of us coming out of the church.

After the ceremony, I remember coming out to the door of the church to have our photos taken, and Tommy was sitting there on his knees, clicking away – I noticed later that Mum wasn't in any of them. Thankfully, however, she was in a few at the reception.

On the church porch steps on our wedding day!

(From left) Brian, Jean, Clive, me, Kim, my friend Beverly, and Mrs. Janes' son, Barry.

Cutting the cake.

Our wedding card from Mr. & Mrs. Janes.

After the ceremony, Clive and I and our attendants went back to Mr. and Mrs. Janes' house, where Tommy took more photos. This was to give our guests time to get from the church to the reception hall at a venue called Dence Park, about ten to fifteen minutes away. We had a lovely afternoon, and we went south to a place near Wollongong for our honeymoon.

Our parents, us and the flower girl, at Dence Park reception. (From left) Dad, David, Mum, Hilda, Clive, me, Kim, Ruby and Leonard.

৪০৩

The Sleep-out

We returned to Clive's parent's place in Cheltenham and moved into a simple one-bedroom shed in their back yard, surrounded by bushland. It was built with fibro walls and a corrugated iron roof that they called a sleep-out. Though it was small compared to a house, it was a suitable start for us, and we shared the laundry and bathroom facilities with his Mum and Dad.

As it turned out, I fell pregnant straight away, with my baby due the following September 1962. Clive's mother was happy for us and excited to have a grandchild from this son of hers, however my mum was slower to come around. It took about a month after our wedding for her attitude towards me to start to change. I wanted Dad to be a part of my new family if not her, too, and it took a few months of us visiting them – at least once or twice a month – for her to warm to me.

***

We didn't have ultrasounds back then so you didn't know what sort of baby you were going to have until it was born. I was a week overdue, and when I felt the early pangs of labour, Clive drove me to *The Poplars* maternity hospital in Epping at five o'clock that afternoon. But it would be a few hours until this baby came along. In those days fathers weren't allowed in the delivery rooms, so Clive had been sent home to wait for the news.

News 1962: American actress Marilyn Monroe dies.

In the meantime, Clive's sister-in-law, Jean (my maid of honour) also came in at about seven o'clock to have her second baby. We were given beds opposite each other in the same ward and Dr. Scilla was our doctor for the births. He was on the age of retirement, and seemed, to me, to be a very old man.

Jean was rushed into the labour ward and gave birth to a son, Ricky, at eleven o'clock: it would be two hours ahead of my baby being born. Dr. Scilla came to see me when Jean was finished.

"Everything's going okay," he said after he'd checked my condition. "I'll see you in the morning."

"Okay," I replied, nervously wondering how things would go.

"Just relax and have a good night's sleep," he said with a smile and left.

But apparently he'd just nicely got home and into bed to get his own sleep when the hospital called him to come back in for me.

"You have to come back in now. Mrs. Duncan is having her baby," they'd said.

"But she's already had it!" he'd replied.

"No, this is the other Mrs. Duncan*."

So he had to turn around and make the twenty to thirty minute drive from Cheltenham to be there for me. However I didn't remember him coming back, all I knew was that I was having these painful contractions.

Unfortunately my baby was in breech position, which meant he was coming out feet-first. The staff had to turn him around, but they had a lot of trouble and couldn't get him into position.

"To make it easier, Mrs. Duncan," they said, "we're going to give you some orange juice with cod liver oil."

* *Footnote: my pen name*

'*No, not that bloody stuff again!*' I thought. It tasted awful but they assured me that it would help him to come out; I wasn't in pain, but I was uncomfortable. They knew it was going to be a boy by this point because they'd had an x-ray of him.

"We're going to take you down to the labour ward," the nurses said, and they helped me out of bed. In those days, they used to put women on a wheeled bed, or in a wheelchair, to get them to the labour ward. But with this being my first baby, and I, not knowing what was happening, they made me walk all the way down to the ward – which seemed like a mile away! I know it was quite a distance all the same.

"We want you to come into the labour ward," they said, coaxing me along. "We're going to give you an enema."

I didn't know what that was, but I soon found out. Basically, they filled my bowel with water. After that they took me to the toilet.

"Now hang on to it," they said. "You've got to hang on tight. Squeeze your bottom as hard as you can."

I soon realised that they were flushing my system of any waste, so that the baby wasn't at risk. And the walking, which they had me do on the return trip, too, was in the hopes of turning the baby from his breech position. When I finally got back to the labour ward and got on the bed, they put a mask on my mouth.

"I don't want the mask!" I said, trying to turn away.

"We're just going to help you have this baby," they insisted, covering me with the mask. I felt some air come in, and then I must have gone out to it, for I don't remember anything after that. The next I knew, the baby was born; I don't know if he was breech-birth, head birth or what. I was half-stoned and don't even remember them asking me what I was going to call him, but for some reason I must have said, "Leo".

So they'd put his name down as Leo, and it was also put on a tag on his bed in the babies' nursery ward – which my mother-in-law saw and was most upset about…

Clive was told the following morning that he'd had a little boy. He came back to see us as soon as he could. We hadn't talked about names for him and as far as I knew, our son was still yet to be given his.

"How come your going to call the baby Leo?" he asked.

I was surprised. I didn't want to call him Leo!

"I'm not going to call him Leo!" I said, puzzled. "It'll be somewhere in his name, but certainly not as his first one!"

"Well, that's what they've got here," he said, indicating the name tag on his cot.

"Well I don't remember giving him that name," I said. "I don't know where they got that from!"

"Well, Mum's very hurt and upset because you told the nurses that you're going to call him Leo."

"I don't remember saying that," I insisted. For the life of me I couldn't recall the conversation with the nurses.

When Clive was about ten years old, his eldest brother, Leo, was killed in a plane crash while testing an aircraft with his job at the Australian Air Force. Although it wasn't specified what actually caused the crash of this six-month-old plane, his death had hit the family very,

very hard. Being the eldest son in an era where first-born males were especially favoured, Ruby had suffered terribly with his loss and was apparently never the same afterwards. So she was very, very hurt at seeing his name for my son, and I think she was upset because I hadn't ask her for her permission.

However a suitable name just didn't seem to come to mind that quickly.

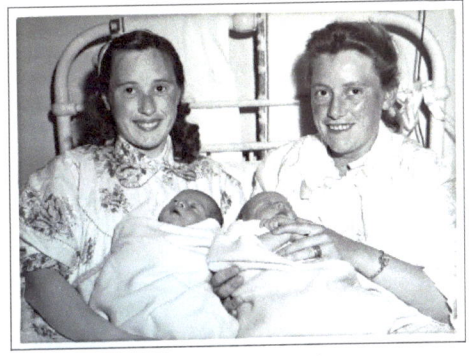

Left: Me with my first-born son, "Leo", and Jean with Ricky (Right).

***

When they brought him up to me to be fed, I looked at his face and thought, *'That's not my baby.'*

I couldn't look at him. To me, he looked like a little baby monkey, or like a cross between a German and a Chinaman. It might sound harsh, but not every mum thinks their baby is beautiful! I couldn't see anything of Clive or myself in his face and I thought that he wasn't mine.

"That's not my little boy!" I said, feeling miserable.

They had to insist that he was mine, but I didn't see him born! As far as I was concerned, they'd tricked me; you would hear sometimes about babies having being accidentally given to the wrong mothers. Hospitals back then had a separate Baby Ward where newborns were kept when they weren't with their mums, and that's how mistakes could be made, especially if the name tags fell off the crib, or were swapped. It took me a couple of months to warm up to him, and maybe that was why finding him a name was so hard!

***

My mum surprised me again. She actually came to the hospital once or twice in the week while I was there! In those days, new mothers had to stay in hospital for at least one week to make sure we knew how to feed, bath and dress the baby. When they were happy with our progress, we were able to go home. Not like today's mums, who go in and out on the same day, unless there are any complications. But then, mums of today are given weeks of prenatal classes, where they learn how to properly care for the baby, as well as having post care services available.

Melancholy is the best way to describe Mum's feeling at the time. Her mood seemed to be, *'Oh well, I got a grandson. I suppose I better see him.'*

She'd already had a granddaughter by now through Hilda, but I'm sure she was still very upset with me for having left home the way I did. And no doubt she still held a grudge against me for marrying a man she didn't approve of (for not being "a good English man"). I think she couldn't stand me being who I was. I don't recall that she held him, either.

I don't remember Dad coming at all. I think he must have been banned by Mum. I'd say if Dad brought her down for the visit, she'd have let him stand at the window of the Baby Ward and who knows, they may have thought, *'Oh yeah, that's him,'* and walked off again. Mum never ever stayed very long at the hospital. When she did come it was a matter of, *'ten minutes, yeah I've seen him, now I'm going home again.'*

In fact for his first couple of years, I don't think she could get used to the idea that I was getting on with my life, and I know she didn't like it. She had no control over me anymore, not after I got married.

༄༅

Finding a Name

About three weeks later, when Clive and I were sitting looking at him in our little sleep-out, we thought of a name for our son.

"What are you going to call him?" Clive asked.

By now, his newborn's face was changing, and he was starting to look like a nice little baby.

Arthur's first baby card.

It still took me a good couple of months to warm to him – I just couldn't get passed the fact that I hadn't *seen* him straight after being born, and therefore I couldn't say definitively that he was *mine*.

I wasn't sure of a suitable name, and I wanted a nice one, a respectable name that people would look up to. I knew a lady who came up from Sydney to visit Mum, and her husband was called Arthur, and he seemed to be a nice, respectable man, so it sort of stuck in my mind.

The baptism booklet for Arthur - price, three pence!

"Well Arthur sounds a nice name. What do you reckon?" I said.

Clive wasn't too convinced.

"Ahh I suppose. It's a bit old though, isn't it?" he replied.

"Yes, well he's gotta grow old, hasn't he?" I playfully quipped.

So we settled on the name Arthur.

"*Now* he can have his name Leo included," I said. "He can be Arthur, Leonard, Clive!"

***

Unfortunately he'd had a difficult start to life, right from the beginning with his breech birth. He had significant health problems during his life, and at just two weeks old, he got so sick that he needed specialist attention.

For the first week he was okay, but when we got him home by the second week, I noticed that he wasn't doing many wet nappies, so we took him along to see Dr. Scilla to tell him what was happening.

"Well sometimes they can go a couple of days to a week," he said. "I wouldn't panic just yet. But keep an eye on it and let us know if there's any changes."

"Well he hasn't done any number two's yet," I said, still concerned.

"Oh that'll come eventually. How are you going feeding him?"

"Well it seems like he brings a lot of stuff up – the milk doesn't seem to go down," I replied.

"That's a concern," he said thoughtfully. "We'll keep an eye on that. If it doesn't settle down by the end of the week," he said, "we'll send you to see the specialist."

But by the end of Arthur's third week, whenever he tried drinking my milk, he'd bring it back up a little bit later. He didn't have any bowel movements and his nappy was mostly dry. By the fourth week he was bleeding and he couldn't keep any food down and was vomiting straight after feeding. It got that bad that he'd barely take it in and it would immediately fly back out across the room, just like a spray or jet of liquid.

I didn't know what to do and I was frightened I was not doing something right for him, so I talked to Dr. Scilla about it.

"He's bleeding now," I explained. "There's spots of blood coming out on his nappy."

"There's something wrong with him, definitely," he said with concern. "We'll have to get him into the Tresillian Home as soon as we can, because he should have been using his bowels by now, and he should not be bleeding."

I was really worried for him and thankfully we were taken into *The Tresillian*, a hospital for women with sick babies, reasonably quickly. They put me in a bed and kept Arthur in the nursery, and monitored us for a week. When they'd bring him around to be fed, the same thing would happen.

"Put this nappy over you in case he's sick," the nurse would say.

As soon as I'd start to feed him, Arthur reacted as though he was choking.

"Well he's had enough now," she'd say, and no sooner had they picked him up, out shot his milk, all over them.

At six weeks old, he was finally diagnosed with *Pyloric Stenosis*. The doctor who was going to see him there came to visit me at around five o'clock that afternoon, and took some time to explain Arthur's situation with me.

"He's going to have to go to Camperdown Children's Hospital," he said. "They specialise in the health of babies and kids. "Now I'm going to show you what's wrong with him, and what we're going to do," he said, and drew a little diagram for me. Then he described the details, using terms I that struggled to understand.

"...This is the area where the little valve is. The food goes in here, the door's supposed to open, the food goes in there, settles down, and comes out the other end; the door will shut. But what your son is doing is – the food is coming in, but the door is shutting, not opening as it should. It's just hitting the door and coming straight back out again because it has nowhere to go. And that's what your problem is with your little boy."

The technical side of it may better describe things as "when an opening between the stomach and small intestine thickens, causing a gastric outlet obstruction", and basically means that a valve leading to the digestive system allows food to enter into the stomach, like a door which opens when food is present and closes when there's nothing to be digested". But for Arthur, his valve closed when food was waiting to go in, causing a build-up that, naturally, had nowhere to go but back up through his mouth.

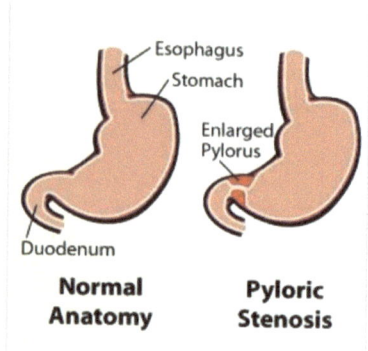

"We're going to take him down to Camperdown Hospital now and around about nine o'clock, we'll be operating on him," he said. "I have other babies to do too, but we'll get to him just as soon as we can."

He must have seen the worried look on my face.

"We've got two ahead of your little boy, but you can come down and see him in the hospital and it'll be alright," he said, and left.

Clive had to drive us there and we left at around eight p.m. Thankfully there was only about ten minutes between the children's hospital and The Tresillian; I don't think I could have endured a longer wait, because when I finally got to see him, boy did I feel like I wanted to cry!

Our poor little baby had tubes in his mouth, up his nose and seemingly everywhere! And he was as white as a white sheet of paper!

"Oh! What's wrong with him!? He's white!" I cried.

"It's alright, Mrs. Duncan," a nurse said. "That's the infection; it's what's bothering him. We're getting him up to surgery very shortly. You can sit in the waiting room if you want, or you can go back to The Tresillian. But as soon as we can get him into theatre, we'll have him looked after."

We chose to wait, and the time seemed to take forever. I was expecting someone to come out and tell us that the operation was all over with by around quarter past or half past nine, as I had no idea what the type of surgery was; if it was complex or reasonably easy. We were so worried about how things were going, not knowing just how serious his situation was. We noticed the clock coming up to eleven p.m. and that's when I found out what had been happening for them.

An emergency had come up for them. It was Arthur's, but they didn't tell me it was him. All we were told is that the doctor had been delayed.

"How is he?" we asked the intern when he finally came out to see us.

"Your son is okay," he gently said. "The doctor is with him now."

"What took so long? Was there any problems?" we asked, frustrated with the unexplained disruption.

The man sort of hesitated.

"We've had to put him on hold as we've had another emergency come in," he said.

"What?!" we cried. "He still hasn't been operated on?!"

"Now don't panic yet!" he added. "Your son is up next and we'll be operating on him at eleven o'clock."

Clive and I feared the worst. I really wanted to demand that he be looked at now!

"He's okay," the intern repeated, trying to keep us calm, "but it'll be a little longer than we expected, and we'll let you know when it's all over. Just relax and go have a cup of tea."

I didn't feel like having a cup of tea. I didn't feel like having anything but our baby back safely in our arms and all healed up.

It was around midnight when the doctor who did the operation came into the waiting room.

"It's okay, we've just finished operating on him now," he said.

We breathed a sigh of relief.

"We got him in time and the operation went well; everything is fine, "Your son is out of danger now."

We didn't know he had been in danger!

"But if we had waited another fifteen minutes," he added cautiously, "it would have been too late, for he would have died."

Our hearts jumped. I *knew* it was a lot worse than they had let on!

(*It was many, many years later that I would learn the truth behind those words – Arthur came to me in a vision in 2017 and said that he had died in that operation, he had stopped breathing for a few minutes just before they were about to start on him. They'd had to work quickly to revive him, and he had fought hard to live!*)

News 1963: American president John F. Kennedy dies.

The doctor didn't want to upset us by telling us all of it.

I was deeply hurt when I learned that I had been lied to, but at the time, we could only go on what we were told.

Arthur's colour finally came back into him after about three or four days.

* * *

Arthur's health continued to give us concerns. He'd no sooner be getting over one illness and he'd be coming down with something else. Literally week by week, months by month he was struggling.

Our first Wedding Anniversary card from Mum, Dad and Brenda.

After his *Pyloric Stenosis* at six weeks old, he then had diarrhoea at twelve weeks, Colic at thirteen weeks, and the German measles at fourteen weeks. When he was five and a half months old, he came down with a bad cold, and later a very bad cold at nine months that nearly turned into pneumonia! And just after that, he got an infection on his penis.

All of these seemed to have had an effect on Clive's Mum, Ruby, as it took so long for her to get used to him. In the meantime, she wanted to do everything for me, including cooking, cleaning and pretty much whatever else she could help herself to. Even before Arthur was born, she would have our meals cooked or our washing done. A couple of times I tried asking her if I could use the washing machine, but her answer was always the same.

"Oh no, it's dangerous," she would say, and the look in her eyes was like, '*I don't want you to use my washing machine*'.

And I couldn't get around it, either. Reusable cloth nappies were what we gave our babies back then, and after each change, I'd put the used nappy in a bucket to soak in the laundry. Every couple of days I'd be ready to wash them, and I'd put Arthur in the pram and walk him down there so he could be with me.

But there was Ruby, already about to hang out the nappies. I'm sure she'd have even bathed him if I hadn't got to it first!

I could have cooked for Clive and I too, all I needed was the stove, for I could prepare the vegetables up in our hut. But when meal time was due, she'd already made the meals and was calling us down to join them. I think she was uncomfortable with me using her things.

So I spent a lot of time in our little hut away from her, frustrated with not being able to do the work I wanted to do. There were many times I would be laying awake on the bed, looking up at the ceiling or the tops of the walls, waiting to see yet another spider up there. With the bush surrounding us, Huntsman spiders were always around and one particularly awful experience was seeing the mother in one corner… and lots of her babies spread everywhere around the rest of the ceiling! We also had to keep a look out for Red back, Trapdoor, Mouse and Funnel Web spiders, as well as snakes! They all thrived in the area.

My cousin Gerry, holding Arthur.

The sleep-out was small and pokey with both our bed and the bassinette in there, along with the wardrobe we had. I fell pregnant again and when Arthur was about nine months old and had got too big for the bassinette, Clive and his father, Leonard, built an extension on the end of this shed. They cut a door in the corner wall to make a separate bedroom for us, and the original first half of the sleep-out became our kitchenette. I was determined to give us as much independence as possible, so Clive bought us a Range Cooker, fridge, and a table with two chairs.

Now I had my own cooking space. The Range Cooker had two burners for the stove and a griller underneath, so the vegies were boiled on the top, and the chops were grilled below. It was wonderful!

Our 'new' bedroom had our double bed, a cot for Arthur, his former bassinette, (now waiting for the second baby) and our wardrobe. It might have been a small place, but it was our home.

I had Arthur potty trained at nine months, too, after which we put him into trainers. Unfortunately Clive's mother was still interfering with things, still insisting on washing our clothes rather than letting me wash and hang up our laundry. I sort of wasn't allowed to even bathe Arthur in the house at some stages, though to her, it might have been because of my pregnancy. Pregnant women were treated like they were fragile back then and we were always encouraged to take things carefully. But this could have been an excuse for her, too, I don't know.

We were eighteen months in the sleep-out, and at about two months before our second baby was due, I was fed up with my mother-in-law being in the way.

"If I don't get out of here," I said to Clive, "I'm going to go mad!"

So we went looking for a house.

As soon as he could walk, Arthur loved following his Dad around. Here he is (in the background), playing with a tap around the corner of Mum and Dad's Dundas house. From Left: Arthur, Max, my cousin Gerry (foreground), and Clive (on right).

Our First Home

In December 1963 we made one of the biggest milestones in a couple's life. We found a package deal being offered with a real estate agency at Wentworthville, which promised nice, affordable houses with a block of land of your choice. There was a new housing estate going up in the Hills district west of Sydney, so we went and had a look.

Our First Home Card.

We found a street that had a gentle slope with only two blocks still available. The rest were sold and there was only one or two other houses already built in it. So we picked the block that suited us best. Clive went to the bank near his work in Sydney to arrange a loan to cover the mortgage, as he'd saved enough money to buy the land and put a deposit down on the house.

In the second week of January 1964, we got the call to say that the builders were going to start work on it. We were so excited that we would go out to see its development every couple of weeks, admiring with each visit how a new part of the house was coming together, or where it was completed. As soon as it was ready in late March, we moved in.

It was our very first home together and it was beautiful! It was modern, too, with three bedrooms, a toilet, shower and bathroom combined, a good-sized kitchen, (with a four-element gas stove) an adjoining dining room, a big loungeroom, and a laundry attached to the back of the house. The yard was fenced down the sides and back and

Clive had a lock-up garage for his car. It was the ideal Aussie dream!

And it was just in time.

Six weeks later, in early May, I went into labour.

Of all places, I was on the toilet when it felt like a lot of pins and

Our very first home!

needles were stabbing me in the groin. I realised that it must have been the baby starting to come, only I didn't recognise it straight away. I had gone there thinking I'd needed to relieve myself, but then I felt this strange sensation, like a tennis ball was wanting to come out. I thought to myself that it wasn't right, the 'ball' was in the wrong passage. I went back to bed and spoke to Clive about it, knowing something was up.

"I don't know what's wrong with me, but I've got this pins and needles feeling in me, and it's like a tennis ball is wanting to come out," I said. I took notice of the time – it was about quarter to five in the morning. I lay down, wondering what I should do.

"I'm going to call the doctor," he said, equally concerned, and left to make the call. We didn't have the telephone connected to the house in those days and he had to jump on the bicycle and ride around the corner to the nearest telephone booth on the main road – over three blocks away. When he came back, he seemed a little calmer.

"Well, I explained to the doctor what you described, and he said that it sounds like you're getting contractions," Clive said. "In fact, he said, "Don't worry about rushing her to the hospital, just have yourself a cup of tea and then get her there as soon as you can." So, you can have a cup of tea if you want?"

"I'm not going anywhere!" I said, as I stood up off the bed. Then I felt something was really happening and so I threw myself back down, reaching for the bed sheet, just in time for the baby to arrive. She came with the birth waters and, with only Clive to assist me and no towels or cloths prepared, the bedspread was our saving grace.

Then Clive rushed next door to our neighbour, Judy, who worked in a general hospital, and she went across the road to get Mrs. Higgs, a lady who worked at Parramatta Hospital. They both hurried over to help me with the newborn baby.

Meanwhile Clive got back on his bike and rode to the telephone booth on the main road to inform the doctor what had happened. He told Dr. Cook that she'd been born, as well as the address he had to come to, which was a forty-five-minute drive for him.

He finally turned up at seven o'clock, an hour later than anticipated. Apparently, he couldn't find our house because it was in a new estate, though Clive had been clear in his directions. He came rushing in with his little medic's bag, took one look at the two ladies in the room with me, and said, "Has either of you got a certificate?"

He was very abrupt from the start, and he looked angry at me, as if I'd woken him up and got him out of bed too early, instead of waiting to go to the hospital like a good woman should.

"Yes," they replied, luckily having brought their papers with them.

"There's my certificate," Mrs. Higgs said, showing him the document. "I'm a Sister at the Maternity ward."

"Good," he said, and took all the particulars down. "And what are you?" he said to Judy.

"Oh I'm just a nurse," she replied.

I thought to myself later that, there was me, relying on her to look after me and my daughter as if she was the experienced one in maternities, when she didn't have anything to do with babies! But she was wonderful in her care.

Mrs. Higgs was a trained sister and midwife and had cut the cord, then handed our little one to Judy to clean and bundle up in a blanket, while she'd tended to my needs. They had also got a little heater on beside me, because I was shivering; according to them, I had gone into shock. They'd put blankets around me, even up around my neck to keep me warm.

After checking the credentials of the two ladies, he *then* came and checked me out.

"Have you got the placenta out yet?" Dr. Cook asked them.

"No, not yet," Mrs. Higgs said. "I've been trying but it won't come."

He came up to me and put his hands out, saying, "We're just going to get this out." Without warning, he firmly squashed down on my lower belly, which solved the issue of the placenta! With Arthur's birth, I had been out to it on the gas, so the experiences of labour and post labour wasn't something I was particularly familiar with.

"Can you go and bury this somewhere?" he said to Clive, who was standing in the background, probably feeling a little lost. "As soon as she's cleaned up, get her to the hospital."

So Clive had to figure out what to do with it and Dr. Cook left. I learned later that he'd got a meat tray for the placenta and buried it down the back yard.

***

We put our new baby in her bassinet, on the back seat of the car, and I sat in the front with Clive. Mrs. Hawley came over just before we were about to leave, and Clive asked her if she could look after Arthur for us until he got back home.

It was around eight-thirty when Clive was driving down the main road to the hospital, when up ahead he saw a policeman in the process of writing out a ticket to a truck driver in the opposite lane. Because he wanted to get us to the hospital as quickly as possible, Clive began tooting the horn to get his attention, but didn't stop.

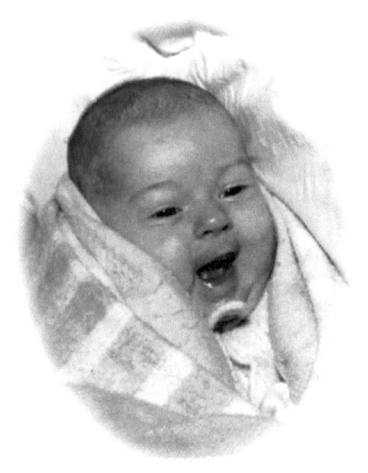

Baby Debbie.

The policeman got on his motorbike and made a U-turn over to our lane, and steadily drove alongside us to see what was wrong. Clive slowed down and they talked through the open window.

"What's the problem?" the policeman called.

"My wife's just had a baby," Clive said. "Can you guide me through the peak traffic to Ryde Hospital please?"

"Yeah no problem," he said. "Follow me and I'll take you."

So we did, but as the policeman drove on, he gradually got further and further ahead of us, and other drivers were cutting us off, filling in the gap between us in their rush to get to work. By the time we got to the other side of Paramatta, which was now a city in itself, the policeman stopped and waited for us to catch up to him.

"I can see we're having a bit of trouble," he said to Clive. "You just get going and I'll follow you instead.

Memories From My Past

So Clive pulled out and around him and drove us the rest of the way as quickly as he could, with the policeman following us, his bright blue lights flashing and the siren blaring. Unfortunately we were now much further away from our destination, and it took us an hour to get there – but can you imagine the looks of the other people watching us as we sped through the traffic? Likely they were thinking, *'Boy, they're in for it now!'*

They had to move over for the policeman and clear the way, and here were we seemingly ignoring the law! Presumably he had informed the police station about our situation so as not to draw fellow police into a false chase.

We finally got to Top Ryde. He must have also radioed ahead to the hospital, as there were nursing staff just out by the main entrance waiting for us. One of them sat me in a wheelchair as the other took our daughter out of the bassinet and put her in my arms. They wheeled us in straight away, as Clive was left to park the car and thank the policeman, who went back to his road patrol. After Clive had seen me safely settled in my ward, he hurried home to Arthur.

***

Although we didn't have things like ultrasound technology back then, and therefore we didn't know if our babies were going to be a boy or a girl, I had hoped this second baby would be a daughter. So I already had her name picked before she was born. My two favourite actresses were Deborah Kerr and Debbie Reynolds, and so she became Deborah, or Debbie for short.

After the week was up and I was allowed to leave hospital, we brought Debbie home. With Debbie's arrival, Mum started to mellow and things began to improve with us. Debbie was a little girl and she was beautiful, and Mum was smitten with her. She thought the sun shone out of her; you could see she was really pleased. It seemed she couldn't stay away from us for too long and wanted to visit a bit more often, making the twenty-minute drive from Dundas, with Dad, at least once or twice a month.

***

My very first try at decorating a cake.

When Debbie was three months old, we had her christened, with a small party of relatives we'd invited to share the day. I attempted to make her a christening cake, which turned out reasonably good for my first go! But Mum couldn't cuddle her enough. It sort of took Debbie's birth to bring the peace together between us and soon, we all began to get along pretty well.

So life was now looking brighter for me as Mum got closer to us. She even watched over the children when Clive and I had to go out, or whenever I was busy, and we returned the favour by taking the children to see them as often as we could.

I guess it needed the children to bring Mum back to liking me again. I think, too, that my new surroundings must have made an impression on her. Starting out, we didn't have a lot of money for furniture and in fact, all we did have was the bare essentials we'd brought with us from the sleep-out, like the cot and bassinette, our double bed, our wardrobe, the table and chairs, some kitchen things and some linen. And she warmed up to Clive in a big way.

"You know, you're doing a very good job, looking after Joyce," she said to him one day. "If you like, I've got an old lounge suite there. If you want it, you can have it."

I nearly fainted!

She ended up giving us the old lounge that folded down into a double bed, plus two nice big comfy recliner chairs as well. Whenever she wanted to stay with us, she slept on this lounge, and couple of months later, my sister Hilda bought us some Venetian blinds to cover all the windows in the house!

℘ﻫ

Debbie's 2nd Birthday card from Mum and Dad (Nan & Pop Duncan)

My Son's Health

Unfortunately, we had only been in our new home for about three months when Arthur's health took another hit. Almost into his second birthday, he got the dreaded Whooping Cough. His coughing got so bad through the night that we brought him into our bed, trying to sooth him. His poor little face turned red and he must have been very sore in his throat. Seeing him like this made me cry and we were frantic that he wouldn't make it to the morning, when the doctor's surgery would be open.

Left: Arthur (about 6 m.o.) and his cousin, Susan (about 11 months)

Right: Arthur (about 2 1/2 y.o.) and Susan (about 3 y.o.)

By six-forty-five a.m. we decided to call the emergency line as his condition had worsened considerably. Clive explained Arthur's situation to the telephone operator and she arranged for a local doctor to come down right away.

I held him close, frightened for the worst. Within fifteen minutes his lips started turning blue.

"Clive!" I called out. "He's turning blue!"

I realised he had stopped breathing. I looked out of the bedroom window, desperately hoping the doctor had arrived. It was right on seven o'clock, and he was there – just in time.

"The doctor's just pulled up out the front!" I yelled to Clive. "Tell him Arthur's stopped breathing! Hurry!"

Clive must have met him at the door, for the next minute, the doctor rushed into our room with his bag. He took out a syringe and put it in Arthur's arm and a moment later, our son took a deep breath.

Our relief was huge and we waited anxiously as the doctor continued checking him over. When he was sure his vitals were good, he gave us medication for Arthur to take every four hours until he returned to normal.

This was the second time I had felt so scared for him, but it would not be the last. The next time was simply horrific.

***

For most people, telephone communication in the early sixties was limited to the public telephone box, (the classic wooden, "red booth") and these could be found at every shopping centre, some petrol stations, and on the side of residential streets every three or four blocks apart, often on the corner.

The house telephone started to become readily available around 1963-'64 and we decided to get it "put on" in September, just after my birthday, in case we had any emergencies with the kids. It turned out to be a sensible idea.

A telephone booth just like the one we used to have.

On Mother's Day in 1965, Mum and Dad had come to visit us. Debbie was twelve months old and Arthur was now three-and-a-half. Our relationship with my parents had been growing, as Mum was coming to love my husband, and Dad had formed a bond of love and respect with him too.

Clive was out in the front yard, working on a retaining wall when he decided to go to the nearest quarry for some sandstone blocks, and Dad offered to go with him to help load the trailer. Neither of them had experience with reversing or turning a box trailer and although Clive has always been a safe driver, he hadn't foreseen what was soon to happen.

Young Arthur idolised his father and wanted to be with him in everything, no matter where he went or what he was doing. Clive had decided to utilise the new neighbour's unused driveway opposite our own to park the car and trailer, where he and my dad planned to unhook the trailer, reverse the car back onto the road, turn the trailer around and re-hook it afterwards.

Arthur had seen his dad and Pop busy out across the street and he'd decided to go after him, running up our driveway without any other thought but his Daddy. At that same time, another neighbour, Basil, who lived on the diagonal corner of our street, was driving home down the hill from church.

No one saw the toddler run onto the road.

Thank goodness Basil was only going slowly. His car drove over the top of him.

Clive turned in time to see him rolling under the car, thinking he was only a cardboard box. But Basil stopped to find out what he'd hit, for he didn't know it was Arthur, either. That's when Clive saw his son, lying motionless, on the ground at the back of the car. He didn't hesitate.

He reached for Arthur, picked him up and jumped straight into Basil's car.

"Take us to the hospital, please!" he shouted. "It's Arthur! You've hit my son!"

Basil was no doubt horrified with the terrible accident and he quickly got back in the driver's seat and raced them off to the hospital.

Meanwhile my dad was speechless with shock. Mum and I were busy inside the house. We had no idea what had just happened. The next we knew, Dad came bursting into the house, out of breath.

"Quick! You've got to come with me to the hospital *now*!" he cried, looking stricken. "Arthur's just been run over!"

"What, how?" I asked, struggling to catch up. "He was just here a couple of minutes ago! How could that happen so quickly?"

"He's run out on to the road just as another car came down. I think he was wanting to be with us," Dad explained. "Come on, we don't have time to stand around. Let me take you to the hospital!"

I looked at Mum, shocked with dread, and vaguely thinking about little Debbie. She must have known what I was thinking.

"You go and I'll stay here and look after Debbie," she said, her face as white as Dad's.

We got into Dad's car as quickly as possible and he drove as fast as he dared get away with to get us there. He was shaking with nerves and pulled up at the main entrance to let me out.

"When you are ready to come on home, ring me and I'll come back and pick you up."

I didn't stop to ask if he wanted to come in with me. I was too numb to say much at all.

"Okay," I replied, and hurried off to find my boy and husband.

I found them eventually; Arthur was in theatre being treated for head wounds and Clive was outside, white as a sheet and tearful.

"How is he?" I asked.

"I don't know," he replied, trembling. "But it's serious."

"What happened?"

He shook his head slowly, still in a daze, I suppose.

"I… don't know. Basil said something about not seeing him run out onto the road, but he heard the thump. He just knew he'd hit something but he didn't know what until he got out to have a look."

Clive's eyes spilled over with tears.

"He hit our son, Joyce!"

We hugged and cried.

"Did he die on the way to hospital? Has he died in here!?" I had to know.

"No," he replied. "I held him all the way. The doctors have him now."

We had to wait a while before any news of his condition came through. When it did, it wasn't pleasant.

"We've got him safe now," the doctor said after the operation had finished. "He'll be alright, but there could be complications down the track."

"Like what?" we asked.

"Well, he's experienced a significant brain injury. He may have memory problems later, or learning difficulties. Anything may arise with damage to the brain."

We were devastated.

"What can we do?" we asked, desperate to hear that he would come through this without any problem.

"You need to keep him quiet and still. Don't let him get too boisterous or run around. And whatever you do, don't let him bump his head! We've bandaged him up, but you have to understand that his brain was hit very hard, and there was a lot of blood and scarred tissue. He has a dent in his skull that will probably even out as he gets older – hopefully."

This was too much to take in.

"You can take him home with you tonight, but like I say, keep him stable for the next few days, even for a couple of weeks. And take him straight to your doctor if you see anything unusual!" Before he walked away, he shook his head in disbelief. "He's a tough little feller – he fought to stay with us. We nearly lost him. But you've got a strong son there."

Later that night we rang home. Dad and Mum were waiting to hear from us.

"Is he okay?" they asked.

"Yes, yes! He's okay, but he's in a very bad way and his head is heavily bandaged," Clive said. "We're bringing him home with us tonight. We're ready to leave the hospital. Please come and get us as soon as you can. We're tired."

Dad drove all of the way in to pick us up, looking at our baby with sadness and being as careful as he could with us, driving home slowly and avoiding any bumps or pot holes as best he could. We arrived at around eight o'clock and carefully bundled our boy into his bed.

Mum looked in on him and, as there was nothing more they could do for us, soon left for their home. I saw to Debbie and Clive decided to sleep next to Arthur in case he woke up through the night, wanting to be there to comfort him if he needed it.

I would learn many years later from Arthur's vision in 2017 that he had died in that accident. He'd died twice; once, briefly, in the car on the way to hospital, and again when in the surgery.

So they had lost him. Clive had been in too much shock to see it at the time, and what the doctor had said wasn't entirely true. I guess they weren't wanting to frighten us – just like the time he'd died as a baby and they didn't tell us everything then, either. He was a lucky boy, yes, but he'd lost a quarter of his brain, too. And he had a hole in the right side of his head for the rest of his life.

Arthur (about 19 months) and I, with a young Tess.

***

I had learned to drive when Debbie was about thirteen months old. When she was a year-and-a-half, Clive had a serious visit to the hospital. He was at work one afternoon when he started feeling pain in his stomach and was sent home. He went to the doctor about it the same day, and from there, he was sent straight to Wentworthville hospital in an ambulance with suspected appendicitis.

I got the phone call from the hospital to tell me that they'd admitted him in, and that I could come in to visit him after the operation. So straight away I called Mum and explained the situation. In the meantime, I went over to our lovely neighbour, Mrs. Hawley, to see if she could look after Arthur and Debbie for me. She was always there for me when I needed her and was more than happy to take the kids, as she found they were very well-behaved children.

I drove to the hospital to find he had peritonitis (a burst appendicitis). The next day, he was taken back into surgery because the stitches had split open.

I learned later that after the first operation, the staff had apparently got him up from the bed too early. A nurse had escorted him to the toilets and waited outside for him. Unfortunately, as he was coming out of the stall, the stitches had parted and he could feel his intestines slipping out. So they rushed him back into surgery, working on him all over again. By the time I got to speak with the doctor, it wasn't good.

"How is he?" I asked.

He shook his head disturbingly.

"It doesn't look good," he said. "We had a problem with him; his appendix burst and the stitches came undone. But we've got him fixed up. He's back in bed now. But it doesn't look good. He's lost a lot of blood… it could be that he might not survive the night."

I was lost with this news.

"You might not have too long with him," the doctor said. "You better go and talk to him."

I went to his bedside, and that's when I saw him – he looked like death warmed up. It was scary; he was as white as a sheet!

'He's not going to make it through!' I thought, taking his hand and giving him a kiss on the cheek. Clive was awake but didn't remember too much of our conversation. I was allowed to stay with him a lot longer than the other visitors were given that night, and just kept talking to him until he started to fall asleep.

"He needs his rest," the doctor said on his return to check on my husband. "You better go now. We'll let you know if anything happens."

I gave him another kiss and left.

The next day I went in and was relieved to see a bit of colour in his face. Somehow he pulled through it alright.

༄༅

(Above) Arthur's fourth birthday card.

(Right) Debbie's 2nd Birthday card.

My card to Clive on our 5th Wedding Anniversary

Another Baby

Two years after Debbie was born, we had another son, Kevin, in July 1966.

On the Wednesday morning, nearly a week before our third child was due, I had to go and see my doctor for my weekly check-up. But this doctor was an idiot.

Kevin on the front lawn (about 6 m.o.)

"You've got no problems," he said. "It's not due until next Tuesday."

But when Saturday morning came, I started feeling some contractions. Clive and I were planning to go to the wedding of one of his brother's that day, at two o'clock, in a suburb of inner Sydney, about a forty-minute drive from our home. So I phoned the surgery and made an appointment to see the doctor first, and got in at eleven o'clock. Naturally I was concerned about having a baby during the wedding.

"Don't worry about it," Dr. Cook said. "You're alright. You can go to the wedding, and have a drink for me."

Trusting his advice, I took Arthur and Debbie to Mum's at Dundas, so she could look after them for us. But she wasn't there when we arrived, and while we waited some five minutes in the hopes of her returning soon, I felt more contractions. I kept feeling as if I was sitting on top of a tennis ball at first, which were the same feelings I'd had with the other two babies.

Then my older sister Hilda turned up unexpectedly.

"What are you doing in Mum's driveway?" she asked curiously.

"Well, we've got to go to a wedding in Sydney," I began, trying to ignore the pain in my body. "We've got to be there for two o'clock, and it's now one o'clock. We're running late and Mum was going to look after the kids for us."

"Well you go on to the wedding and I'll look after them for you," she said, just as I almost cried out from another spasm below, and I drew my feet up underneath me to hold it together.

"What's the matter?" she asked anxiously. "Are you alright?"

"Yeah I just keep getting these – ahh! Ahh! – I just keep getting these – ah-ah-ah! – pains running up my back," I tried to say.

"You're in labour," she said with certainty.

"No, the doctor says I'm alright to keep going 'til Tuesday."

"Bugger what the doctor said! I would suggest you go to the hospital *now*!"

"I can't," I said determinedly. "I'm going to the wedding!"

Hilda turned to Clive.

"Don't worry what the doctor said," she insisted, "I *know* she's in labour. *Get* her to the hospital now!"

The hospital was only about ten to fifteen minutes away, and so he took notice of the advice and drove me straight there. We got to the hospital right on one-fifty, and I thought, *'Gosh, we're never going to make it to the wedding!'*

Part of my concern about us being there for his brother was because Clive was to be their photographer.

"I might have to leave you here, Joyce, and carry on to the church, because they need me," he said as he parked the car.

So he got me into the reception area where a Sister met us, and on explaining my situation, she rushed me straight to the labour ward.

"You're due any second!" they said as I came in.

"But the doctor said-" I started.

"Bugger what the doctor said," she cut in. "You're in labour and your sister was right. Get up on that bed."

She examined me to find I was apparently about three or four centimetres dilated, so they tried calling Dr. Cook – who ignored them. They tried again and got through. Apparently he didn't believe what they said.

"But we've got Mrs. Duncan here in the hospital now!" I heard the Sister saying to him. "And she's in labour! And the baby is due to be born any minute!"

He gave a grunt and a groan and hung up, leaving us to wonder if he was going to show up at all. He was based in Epping, which I'm sure was probably about less than twenty minutes away from the hospital, but which he could do in ten minutes.

Right on two o'clock, my new baby started pushing his way out.

"Hang on Mrs. Duncan! Hang on!" they called.

"I can't hang on any longer!" I cried desperately.

As my new son was being born, Dr. Cook walked in the door. He gave a bit of a grunt.

"Oh hello Dr. Cook," I said sarcastically, "can I wrap the baby up and take it to the wedding?"

"No!" he grumbled, then went about checking the baby over.

I had to have four stitches and, in those days, that meant staying in hospital for seven days' recovery.

It turned out that Clive was half an hour late for the wedding, which didn't make the couple very happy. But if I had of taken notice of my then doctor and gone straight to the service, the minister would have been saying, "Does anyone have anything to say about this couple..." – and I would've been yelling out, "Yes! Me!" and our son would have been born right there in the church! Which I'm sure would have made the headlines!

***

TETRA
is the new Filling Material for bedding developed in Australia in 1951 after scientific research on native raw material.
It is made by cleansing, flaking and processing Ti-Tree Bark to rid it of all impurities and non-resilient fibre.
The stripping of the bark does not harm the tree.

When Kevin was only about three months old, I made one of the worst decisions in my life. But I had trusted the people involved and allowed my children to be watched over by them.

This particular day, Clive and I had an appointment to go to and we had no one to look after the kids. My brother and his then-wife, Val, was living with Mum and Dad at the time, and offered to help out. These two were very heavy drinkers and smokers, whereas we were tea-totallers.

"Leave them here with us," she said. "We will look after them."

We were gone for maybe about an hour – that's all it took to nearly kill him.

When we returned, we found Arthur and Debbie playing on the floor with her two children, and Val had Kevin on her knee, holding him as if she were feeding him a bottle of milk. But it wasn't milk.

She had a stubby bottle of beer to his mouth.

"What on earth are you doing?" I demanded.

"Oh he was starting to cry, so I thought I'd give him a drink," she said.

A family dinner. From Left: Val, David, Me, Clive, Allan, Hilda, Mum, Dad, Brenda.

"But that's alcohol!" I exclaimed. "What are you doing giving him that?!"

"Oh it's alright, it'll make him sleep," she happily replied. "It won't hurt him."

I was furious.

"Stop it now!" I demanded. "We don't drink beer and we're going home!"

Unfortunately Mum wasn't there at the time, and if she had of been, I know she would not have let them give him the alcohol in the first place. I went to take him from Val, but she insisted that little Kevin was alright.

"It's alright!" she went on. "Don't worry about him!"

We gathered up the other two kids and left straight away. However worse was to come. I had a hell of a time trying to settle him down at home. He was crying and vomiting most of the time; it worried the hell out of me as I didn't know what to do. I was certain it was because of the drink she'd given him. His eyes started going funny.

The next day, he was very, very red in the face and his eyes were going from side to side, moving separately of each other – literally up and down in opposite directions! I couldn't help but be worried about it, so I rang the local doctor's surgery (*not* the idiot doctor I'd had before) and asked if he could come out to the house to check him.

After the dreadful behaviour of Dr. Cook, I changed surgeries for a more local one at Northmead, where a *much* nicer doctor, Dr. Graham, looked after us.

"He doesn't look too good and I think there's something wrong with him," I said, practically begging him to step through the phone. He came out as soon as he could, and on examining him, he was horrified.

"What the *hell* have you been giving to this baby?!" he asked.

"Well, I haven't been giving him anything!" I answered. "My husband and I went out yesterday and left the kids with my sister-in-law. When we came back, I found her feeding him a bottle of beer!"

"Oh my God!" he moaned and looked at me. "This is the most drunkest child I've ever seen in my whole life! He's had way more than one bottle of beer."

I nearly collapsed. Dr. Graham took pains to explain things carefully to me.

"This child could have toxic poisoning in him. She could have killed him. Did she finish the bottle off?"

"No, thank God," I quickly answered. "The bottle was about three-quarters empty. There was about another quarter of the bottle to go."

He shook his head, bewildered.

"That is the most stupidest thing," he began, but I was getting quite anxious by now.

"Well she told me that she gives it to her kids and it settles them down. But my sister-in-law and brother drink like a fish. Clive and I *don't* drink like fish. We don't even like alcohol!"

"No, that's the trouble," he said, agreeing. "You're going to have problems with this baby. He's either going to end up brain-damaged or he'll have infections. I'll want to check up on him. I'll give you this prescription at the moment. Give it to him as often as you can. Make it three times a day. Hopefully it'll settle him down and we can stop the toxins getting into his system."

It turned out, according to the doctor, that he could have skin rashes, eczema, and even impetigo (*im-peh-tie-go*; a bacterial infection of the skin, most common in young children).

"And if that happens," he said of the impetigo, "I want to know straight away."

By the end of the week he started to come out in little rashes. So I took him straight down to Dr. Graham.

"We'll give you this cream and put it on him," he said, "because if those blisters break, it'll spread all over his body."

But it was already too late. It was already spreading over his little body. Even as I write about this, I'm filling up with hurt.

Dr. Graham sent us to a specialist in Parramatta, where he was prescribed a green-coloured thick cream, that was smothered all over his body, and we had to then wrap him up like a Mummy; all you could see was his face. And even then I had to wipe it all over his face, but I had to also wrap up his hands in mittens because he kept wanting to scratch his rash all the time.

"He will out-grow it," the doctor said, "but it could be say, seven years."

(Right) Kevin's first Christmas, and the rash is still there.

Seventeen years later, he was finally out-growing it.

Even though after seven years he out-grew the worst of it, we still had to take him to a skin specialist to have a test done. There, they put nine marks on his arm, ranging from the smallest to the worst one. From that, they could determine that he was allergic to several foods, including eggs, tomatoes and tomato sauce, orange juice and anything acidic. One of the top ones though, was cats.

"Don't let him go anywhere near cats," the specialist explained.

"Well I've got a little cat now," I said. "We've had it for about two years now."

"Well get rid of it."

"I can't! I've had it since it was a baby."

Having this cat didn't last anyhow, as one of our neighbours was found to be baiting cats, so I lost it within a couple of weeks of this diagnosis. Poor Kevin would break out in a terrible rash anytime he came near a cat.

The second-top allergy he was not to have under any circumstances was alcohol.

"Don't, whatever you do, give him alcohol," he said. "If you give him alcohol, or he smells alcohol, he could die from it. This is the worst case that I have seen. Keep him wrapped up as best you can."

This poor little boy suffered so much for so long because of that drink. He was playing up one day and I went to pick him up, saying, "It's alright Darling," but I didn't get to finish. He was so upset, so cranky, that he picked up a toddler's cane chair by the leg and threw it at Clive, as if to say it was his father's fault.

He only responded to me during the day, but at night, Clive had to sleep with him to keep him calm, because he was crying most of the time. For the first two years Clive had to sleep with him in his bed, and at one point, Kevin had tried to kick his dad out; he didn't like him, and he didn't want him, and that upset Clive very much. It got that way that Kevin didn't even want me.

I think the rash was so irritating, he was lashing out at anybody. I felt so sorry for him, and it took me years to get him over it. At around age five, he got asthma, and so his breathing was something else to be careful about. I could've killed that woman, I was so angry, so hurt that she'd done that to my son!

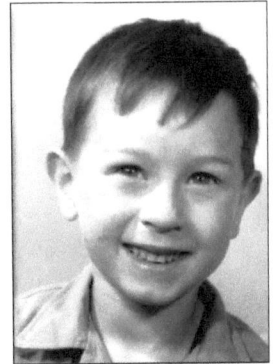

Kevin (about 4 ½ y.o.) with a few lumps still visible.

Even today there are some foods he still can't have, although there are some allergies that he's managed to out-grow. To this day I don't think he's ever been near a cat. My sister, Hilda, who loved cats, got cranky with him one day when he was about eight or nine and she saw him try to scare away one of her cats by kicking out his foot.

"You don't have to do that!" she yelled at him angrily.

I looked at her, just as cranky. I had already told her about his allergies.

"Well the cat shouldn't be near him!" I said. "And sure the cat doesn't know any better, but Kevin knows he's not allowed to be near any cat. If he didn't ask one of us to move the cat out of the road, and it rubbed against him, he would break out in a rash."

It didn't seem to matter to her, she insisted on him not having to be "so cruel" about it, but she just didn't understand. I wanted to go and strangle Val for all of the suffering and hurt he was going through. He was bullied relentlessly at school for the many ways he had to be careful to avoid things.

Even to washing up, he couldn't do it. I can remember his sister, Debbie, saying to me one day, "Why can't Kevin help me wash up?"

It took me straight back to the same sort of scenario of when my mum went off at me when I was younger – when she threw me down on the concrete floor and started bashing my head against it. Brenda was about nine years old when I'd asked if she could help me – well Kevin was now the same age. The soapy water would simply cause his skin to react.

My poor son went through hell for at least the first seven years of his life. There were times where he couldn't breathe properly and was wheezing heavily because a neighbour's cat had come into the yard, and its fur was left lying around. That's when he developed bronchitis.

Whenever he got a cold, he would wheeze to the point of almost losing his breath, and we'd have to get the inhaler to him. He's never been one hundred percent since, and now into his fifties, he has to be careful when handling tools, for if a cat has brushed up against them, his hands break out and he has to get medicated cream on them.

All I can say is that, if you are nursing a child that is from a non-drinking family, *don't* ever give them alcohol! If you are a drinker, or if you're pregnant or feeding your baby, *don't* ever give them alcohol, (or drugs) either – or you will have problems with that child for the rest of their life!

☼☼

Dad, I Love You

In 1968 Dad lost his job as a fitter and turner for large machines. He'd told Mum and us that it was because he'd broken a tool, but Clive learned later on, in a private chat, that he'd been retrenched. He was fifty-five and his prospects of getting another job were poor. His health went downhill quickly after that, and he must have felt bad that he wasn't bringing in the money for his family.

One day in November he had to go out in his car to get something. He was driving along a through-road not far from their house in which he had the right-of-way. But as he neared a T-junction on his left, a driver suddenly appeared and pulled out in front of him. They were supposed to have given way in that instance, but hadn't. Dad's car was hit and nearly rolled, and was damaged beyond repair. Though he survived, the other driver left the scene without stopping.

Mum beside Dad's Singer Gazelle (not long before the accident).

Around two weeks after the accident, Dad began having trouble with his eyes. He was seeing black spots, and eventually he went to the doctor to see what was causing it. He was sent on to the hospital, where he was given tests that indicated he had something wrong with his kidneys. Pretty soon he was admitted in as a patient with kidney failure.

I was four weeks pregnant with my fourth child when we went to visit him in the beginning of December, though no one else knew except for

Clive. I remember every time we went to see him, he was upset. Dad always loved to put up the Christmas lights and streamers at this time of year, but being in hospital meant that he couldn't.

"What's the matter?" I asked him.

"Ohh," he began, semi crying, "I want to get home and put the streamers up. There's no one to put the streamers up!"

It broke my heart.

"No, don't worry," I said determinedly. "We'll help with that."

I told Mum about it and soon everyone in the family pitched in, putting up the streamers and decorations for him, all of us thinking he was still coming home for Christmas.

Clive and I returned with Mum and Hilda every day to see how he was going.

"David and Hilda came around to see Mum the other day," I said. "Clive and I were there with the kids, too - even Brenda turned up!"

"Oh?" he replied, curious.

"Yes, we've got a surprise for you," I said, getting a bit excited. "We've got your streamers up! And all the Christmas decorations too!"

"That's wonderful, Pet!" he said, smiling.

"We can't wait for you to come home for Christmas!"

But Christmas came, then it was New Year, with Dad still in hospital. Sadly his condition had seriously declined in just a few days, and I got a shock to see him.

He had tubes up his nose and down the back of his throat to feed him, which restricted his ability to talk. He was tired and seemed unable to respond to us. On the twelfth of January, Mum was so distressed with his state that she couldn't deal with it and decided to go home with Hilda for lunch. But Clive and I stayed back to keep him company, and I'm so glad we did.

I tried talking to him for about ten minutes as best I could, but it felt frustrating and difficult, and I know it must have been hard for him to answer me, too. Then I remembered a cowboy movie I had seen that had a man who couldn't talk in it, and there was a lady who needed answers from him. She found a way of communicating with him by asking specific questions and having him blink in response. This was a chance for me to try much the same thing, too.

"Dad," I said, "I would like to try something. I know you can hear me, so please blink once for 'yes' and twice for 'no'." I then asked, "Are you comfortable?"

He slowly blinked once.

"Do you think you are going to get better soon?"

He struggled to blink twice as tears filled his eyes. It hurt to see those tears run down the side of his face. I reached for a tissue to dry them, trying not to cry myself.

"I'm so glad we seem to have worked this out," I said, smiling, gently wiping his cheek.

I wanted to keep the conversation going and I could tell he was enjoying my company, so I found other things to talk about, asking him a question here and there that was easy enough for him to blink to. I didn't tell him about my new baby on the way though. We talked for a little while longer, but I could see he wasn't up to it. He was just so sad; he knew he wasn't going to come home.

Mum returned about two hours later.

Dad was smiling a little and I could sense he wanted me to tell her of our breakthrough.

"I have something good to tell you," I said to her as she bent over Dad to give him a kiss on the cheek.

"Oh?" she said, giving us a smile.

"We can communicate with Dad for you!"

She reacted immediately.

"How can you when he can't talk properly!?" she insisted in a huff. "Don't be silly!"

I looked down at Dad. His face had turned unhappy.

"Look, I'll show you," I said, keen to prove it. "If you ask him a 'yes' question, he'll blink once, and if you ask him a 'no' question, he'll blink twice. Watch." I turned to Dad. "Blink once to show Mum how we have worked out how to communicate," I asked him.

He managed to give a very slow, single blink.

Mum was watching him. "How do you know he wasn't blinking normally? How can you tell he was answering you?" she said, clearly doubting us.

"Were you blinking normally?" I asked him.

He struggled to blink twice in answer.

Mum bristled even more.

"Oh that's not talking!" she snappily remarked.

Tears rolled down my father's now very sad face. I can still vividly see it today – I wanted to cry for him, I believed I knew exactly how he was feeling. When we caught each other's eyes, I could see he was wanting to say, *'Don't worry, she doesn't want to understand. So don't even try it again, okay?*' I could feel it; I knew that's what he was thinking.

"Don't worry, Dad," I said to him as he squeezed my hand, "we understand. We'll just talk to you between ourselves."

So I wiped away his tears and continued to talk to him as usual, until Mum realised I wasn't joking. I felt that after about half an hour of this, she saw what was happening and was sort of wanting to believe it was true.

When dinner time came, we decided to leave.

"Love you Dad, see you tomorrow," I said, leaning down to kiss him. "Hope you'll feel better then."

His eyes filled again, and his smile of love was saying "thank you". I firmly held his hand, not really wanting to let go.

"Goodnight," I whispered, expecting to see him again the next day.

The next morning around nine, Hilda and her two children arrived at our place with Mum. We all had important things to do in the city and so Clive was driving us in, after which we would return to the hospital to visit Dad again.

So along with our three children, we piled into our small *Singer Gazelle*; Hilda and Mum with three kids in the back seat; me, Kevin, Arthur and Clive in the front bench seat. Small children were allowed to be sat on the lap in both front and back seats in those days, and seat belts weren't heard of, either.

We headed off to Sydney, which was a forty-minute drive from our place back then, and we got Mum to her appointment at ten o'clock and saw to our own business. Around two that afternoon, we were finally on our way to Top Ryde Hospital to see Dad.

Unfortunately it was now close to peak-hour traffic on the roads out from the city, so the driving was slow. At about ten minutes on, we were stopped at a busy intersection in Balmain, with the hospital still around thirty minutes away. The waiting was very frustrating on us all. It was hot and dry, with no built-in air-conditioning – that was yet to come in future cars.

Suddenly I felt this cold, but gentle kiss on my right cheek.

I looked at Clive, sitting in the driver's seat. He was touching his left cheek.

"Did you feel that?" I quietly whispered to him, hoping the others in the back seat wouldn't hear us.

His face went white. "Yes," he answered.

"Dad, quick!" we both said, instinctively feeling the kiss was from him.

As soon as the lights turned green, Clive put his foot down and sped through the traffic as fast as he could safely get away with. As soon as we parked the car at the hospital, Mum, Hilda and Clive raced off, leaving me behind to look after the kids. I don't know what must have been going through my husband's mind, but I felt so hurt that they'd simply rushed off like that. I wanted to go too of course! After all, it *was* my Dad!

But Clive must have asked the staff to see to me, for about ten minutes later a smallish young nurse appeared from the building and walked towards me. When she was close enough, she broke the bad news that I knew was coming.

"I'm sorry, Mrs. Duncan, but your father has passed away," she gently said.

"How long ago did he pass?" I asked.

"About twenty minutes ago," she said.

I worked it out in my head – with the speed Clive had given to the drive, that estimated thirty minutes would have reduced to twenty. This timed in perfectly with the icy cold kiss on our cheeks. I knew then that it was Dad's way of saying goodbye to us.

"Go on up to be with your family," she said. "I'll keep an eye on the kids for you."

I was so grateful that someone had come to help me! Society was so much friendlier back then, safer, and more trustworthy. So I headed for the lifts and went straight to Dad's ward.

I reached my husband, Mum and sister in the hall outside the lift area of his floor, where they were in a little huddle of hugs and tears. None of them saw me get out of the lift, or stride right past them to Dad's bedside. I was livid with them for just abandoning me like that!

On my own I stood there quietly looking at him, wishing he could open his eyes and we could talk once more.

Just once more, at least.

"I'm sorry Dad," I whispered. "I'm sorry I couldn't be there for you when you passed away. I'm sorry you weren't able to get better and come home and see the streamers and Christmas decorations." I touched his face, remembering where his tears had fallen only the previous afternoon. "I'm glad we had found a way to communicate before you left us. I got your kiss on my cheek," I added with a little smile. I then leaned down and softly gave him a kiss on his forehead in return.

"I love you."

But Mum had just walked in and seen me.

"Oh! Joyce!" she yelled hysterically. "You gave him a kiss! I didn't give him a kiss!"

She came running over to him as I stepped back to leave for the kids. I was very hurt with their behaviour and too upset to care how she felt. As I walked away, she was busily trying to give Dad a kiss too, but I think a nurse was holding her back, because she thought she was trying to climb into bed with Dad. But she was too short to reach him at his bedside. As soon as the nurse understood what she was wanting to do, she lowered the bed's handrail and Mum was able to kiss him on his cheek.

I returned back to the car and thanked the young nurse who had kindly stayed with my kids, and waited for the others to come down, too.

In my heart I was sad that I would not see my beloved Dad again, and that I never got to tell him that I was expecting our fourth baby.

But something inside me told me he already knew.

My beautiful Dad.

A Peek-a-Boo Baby

When Debbie turned five in May of 1969, I made her a birthday cake, which was my very first cake made from a packet mix, (her christening cake had been premade and I had only to decorate it). This one I decorated into a maypole, with a pink musk stick as the pole, five ribbons that trailed down to the mini dolls (dressed as girls, as if holding them), with an icing star on the top of the pole and green icing for the grass underfoot.

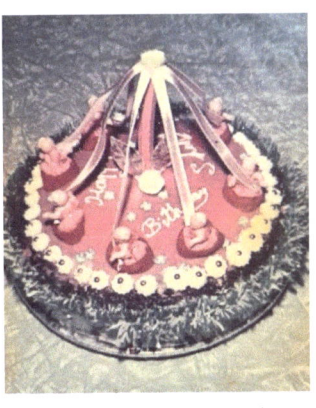

Debbie's birthday cake.

Everyone who came to her birthday loved it, and several of the mothers asked me if I would make their children's cakes too! I was so happy with the positive response that I thought, why not? So I said yes, and had eight decorated cakes to make over the coming weeks, in the same maypole design but in different shades according to the child's favourite colour.

My actual cake order book.

And from that one cake, that became eight, I soon had orders for more coming out of my ears, not just for children's cakes, but for all ages and occasions! I was taken by surprise just how quickly it took off and I was thrilled that they paid me for them too, which helped towards paying for my kid's school things, or their clothes or toys.

My name must have been getting about town, as within two years, I was inundated with lots of cake orders.

Mrs. Hawley helped me out by giving me a recipe for new icing, called *Royal Icing*, which I had not heard of, and it made a big difference to the quality and finish of the cakes. I soon branched into making all kinds of cakes – you named it, I did them, including engagement and wedding cakes, and even novelty cakes like a bridal doll, a record, and a tin of paint!

***

News 1969: Men land on the moon.

In August 1969, seven months after Dad had passed, our fourth baby was born. We had a new doctor in our surgery who I had now been seeing more often than Dr. Graham. At around two in the morning, when I felt the early contractions, Clive contacted the emergency department to alert Dr. Christie for me. By now we had a telephone in the house, and after receiving his call, Dr. Christie phoned us back.

"What route are you taking?" he asked Clive, who was preparing to take me in to the hospital.

Clive told him the roads he would use.

"Okay," he said, "Well, I'm going to get going now and if you're not in the hospital when I get there, I'll come back looking for you."

Knowing how my last two babies had come very quickly, Clive ran over to Mr. and Mrs. Powell's, the neighbours across the road, and asked them if they could look after the kids for us while we were out.

They wouldn't have been a problem as they were sleeping, but it was reassuring to know that a responsible adult was in the house with them all the same. So Mr. Powell quickly put his dressing gown on and came over, and sat on the reclining armchair in the loungeroom as Clive helped me out to the car.

We got to the hospital, right behind our doctor!

"Oh good, you're here!" he said with a smile and took us through to the labour ward. Clive waited with me for only a few minutes, before going back home to check on the kids.

I was able to walk – just, as I could feel the baby coming – and got up onto the bed as a nurse came in to help him. He started looking for it straight away.

"Yes, it's definitely coming," he said encouragingly.

"Well I hope so," I said, "'Cos it's annoying me. I can't shake the feeling of slight pains all the time!"

I was lying there with my hands behind my head, wanting this little one to hurry up.

"Just relax. The baby will be here in a minute - Oh here it comes!" he said, and then, "Oh, it's gone back in again."

I tried relaxing to help with the delivery.

"Oh here it comes!" he cried again, then said, "Oh, no, it's gone back in again."

This happened a few times. Every time he touched the baby's head, it would go back in again.

"This is ridiculous," he ended up saying. "It's not going to come. It must be frightened of me," he joked. "We'll just have a look and see if we can help it out."

He brought out what looked like a giant pair of tongs and just as he saw the head coming back out again, he went to try and grab it.

"Ahh!" he complained.

The baby had slipped back inside.

"Well, at least we know what colour the hair is!" he said, smiling as he held up several tiny hairs on the end of the tongs. "Brown!" He put the tongs aside. "Look, I tell you what," he went on, "This is not going to be easy. Obviously, this baby does not want to be born. No, it wants to be born," he corrected himself, "but it obviously doesn't like me! I'm going to go out and have a cup of tea. And when I come back, we'll try it again. I won't be long!"

Again, I don't remember seeing a nurse in the room and Dr. Christie seemed to be gone for a good five or ten minutes, but in that space, my baby's head decided to come out. As he walked in the door I said, "It's here!"

"Oh good!" he said cheerfully. "Now we can finish it off!" And he wasted no time in grabbing the head and pulling it out the rest of the way, saying, "You're not going back in now!"

When the little one was finally born, he held her, smiling, and said, "Thank goodness it's all over! It's a girl!"

She came into the world at two-forty a.m. We've joked all these years later that, with her popping in and out at birth, that she didn't like men back then! He got the nurse to clean her up and take her off to be weighed, and took me down to a ward. When she was ready to be given back to me, they brought her in, placing her gently in my arms.

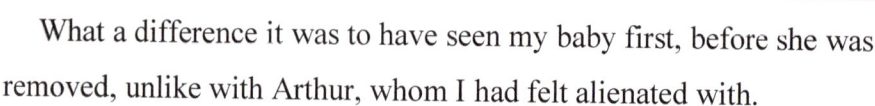

What a difference it was to have seen my baby first, before she was removed, unlike with Arthur, whom I had felt alienated with.

"Okay, I want you to get some rest," Dr. Christie said, "and we'll look after her for now. You'll see her again in the morning."

***

We had her home for about a week and still didn't have a satisfying name for her, thanks to young Arthur. I liked the name Christine, which I had been giving her since she was born. I also had liked Dr. Christie, he was a very good doctor, nice, gentle and had a good way of talking to you – more like a big brother in his manner, and I wanted to call her after him. Plus I liked the name Chrystal, and I nearly called her that, too.

However, Arthur, now almost seven, and who was very excited about this new baby coming into the family, had badly wanted a little sister. Every day he would sit by her bassinette, looking down at her lovingly.

"Oh Mum, she looks just like a beautiful flower," he said one day. "Can we call her Karen, please?"

"Why?" I asked him.

"Because I like that name from the little girl, Karen, on the Mickey Mouse Club. And I want that to be her name!"

Yes, he was in love with Karen (who was paired with Cubby), and because I loved him, I said, "Yes, okay Sweetheart."

The Mouseketeers, with Karen 2nd from bottom.

A few nights later I was preparing the vegetables for dinner, and Karen was crying in the lounge room.

"Sweetheart," I said to Arthur, "can you please put a dummy in her mouth?"

I continued with the vegetables, not thinking much more about it, when after a few minutes I noticed she'd gone quiet, and I heard this lovely little voice singing *Edelweiss* – it sounded just like a little angel singing. It was Arthur, and he sang the whole song through to the end.

"That was beautiful, Sweetheart!" I said when he'd finished. "Where did you learn that song?"

"We were taught it in school today," he said.

My goodness, he'd only learned it that afternoon, and he sang it with all of his heart, putting his little sister to sleep! She looked so peaceful, too! I was so proud of him.

***

She remained as Karen for the next few years – until when she turned five and started school; her class already had about four girls called Karen, and only one girl called Kristina, so the teachers gave her a choice and asked her what she wanted to be called.

"Christine," she said, and won! She was called Christine at school, but because Arthur had so wanted Karen, she answered to that name at home. And just to add some confusion, some years she changed her name back to Karen at school, and would then change it again to Christine the next year. She kept the name Karen as an adult until finally returning to her preferred name, Christine, in around her thirties.

Karen, about 1 y.o.

ಲ‍ಬ

When I fell pregnant with my fifth baby in around 1971, I worried that it would be a boy. This was because both Arthur and Kevin were having significant health problems from their early experiences, and I feared that another son would also be sickly. I kept praying to Spirit… "Please Dad, angels, God – anybody who is listening – if I'm going to have a boy, please don't let me have it! If it's going to be a girl, I'll have it. But I don't want a little boy to be as sick as my other two boys are."

A woman was staying with Mum at the time, she was either a friend of hers, or a cousin. She had come out from England, and was now wanting to move from one house to another house.

"Can you go and help her," Mum had asked me.

I was only in the early stages of pregnancy, about two-and-a-half months in, but I didn't tell anybody about it, not even Mum. So I went to this woman's house to help out.

"Can you take this suitcase?" she asked.

I should have said no. I was told that in the early stages, you shouldn't do any heavy lifting. But I felt that I couldn't tell her that I was pregnant, so I picked up the heavy suitcase and I felt something snap inside. It felt just like somebody had stabbed me with a knife.

About a week later I went to see Dr. Graham.

"I think I've lost this baby," I told him.

"Why's that?" he asked.

So I told him what had happened.

"Oh no," he said unconcernedly, "you can still carry it a week later."

Back home and I started bleeding, so I had another visit with him.

"No I've known people to go through a normal period and still have a baby," he said.

But at ten o'clock one night, Clive had to call the surgery's emergency number to contact my doctor. He rang us back as soon as he got the message.

"She's in a lot of pain," he explained to Dr. Graham. "She's curled up on the floor, crying."

So he came out to our place as quickly as he could.

I was walking slowly around our bed when I felt something come out of me and hit the floor.

"Clive!" I yelled.

Clive rushed in.

"What's up?" he asked.

I was teary. "I've just dropped something on the floor, and I think it's the baby!" I cried.

Dr. Graham came in just behind him, and picked it up.

"Yes," he said, "it's the foetus." He turned to Clive and asked, "Have you got something to put this in? Perhaps a meat tray? That will do well enough."

Clive found out a meat tray and gave it to him.

"Can you dispose of this?" Dr. Graham asked him.

Poor Clive, he had to take this little ball of undeveloped baby outside and bury it in the back yard.

It was too early to have known what sex it was, but I think that if I was going to have had that little baby, it would have been a boy, because I'd prayed that if it was going to be a boy, I didn't want it. If it hadn't been for that woman who wanted me to pick up her heavy suitcase, I wouldn't have lost it. It's interesting for me that back when I was about fifteen, I'd had a very clear vision that I would have four children when I was older, and that they would be a son, then a daughter, then another son, and then another daughter – in that order. And that's all I did have in the end.

***

My boy, girl, boy, girl – as I'd predicted!

*My beautiful kids,
Christmas 1972.*

The Crash that Killed Me

Around December 1973, when Christine was four years old, I had a very bad car accident. I had been looking after another little girl, called Debbie, and she and Christine were in the back seat of our car as I drove us home from the shops late one Friday afternoon.

Clive's Singer Gazelle – the car of my accident.

But just before a crest on the hill, (just on the down-hill slope) I struck an oily slip on the road. I automatically tried to brake, which caused the back wheels to slide, making the car fish tail. Then I hit the curb and mounted the footpath, smashing straight into a telegraph pole. The car had completely turned around and was facing back in the direction of the shops where I had just come from.

We didn't have seat belts in those days, so there'd been nothing to hold me back on impact. I didn't know it, but my head had hit the metal part of the sun-visor, splitting my forehead open. Apparently I had ended up leaning backwards over the bucket-style front seat, with my head almost touching the back seat.

All I remember is feeling very strange, seeing everything starting to fade as a darkness surrounded me, and a circle of light that grew into a tunnel, or an arch at the end of the road. Then I blacked out.

From what I was told later, I had actually died. The accident had happened right out the front of an orphanage and the women inside there came running out to help us, while others might have joined them, because after the girls were taken from the car, someone had also pulled me over the front seat into the back seat.

Thankfully both girls were alright – they had been thrown from side to side in the wild swishing and Christine's chin, apparently, had hit the front bench seat, but they were otherwise okay.

The ladies from the orphanage had also brought lots of cloth nappies with them to bathe my head, as it was covered with blood. When I came to, I thought I was on my lounge at home, and had dozed off for a little while!

'What the hell are all these people doing in the lounge room?' I thought, looking at them.

"How are you feeling, Love?" a man said. He was a paramedic, holding me while bathing my head.

"Good," I replied. "What's happened?"

"You've just had a little accident," he gently said. "You have a cut on your head and will possibly need a couple of band-aids on it."

The dress I was wearing in my accident; with all my hair. This picture was taken not long before my accident.

I tried to reach up to my forehead, as I could feel a warm trickle, but he discouraged that and continued trying to keep me calm.

"Or you might have to have a little stitch and a bandage put on your head," he went on. I believed them, not being able to see what they could see.

And what they could see was horrifying – my forehead had been split open and the scalp had been peeled backward in the impact, exposing my brain. I thought the paramedic was washing my head with warm water, but it was really my blood I could feel! The impact was so hard that the driver's wheel had imprinted on my belly, too.

I tilted my head a bit, looking for the girls, and saw them being held by a couple of women by the kerb.

"How are the girls?" I asked.

"They're alright. They're being looked after."

A policeman was standing outside the car, needing some information from me.

"Do you have your husband's telephone number with you?" he asked.

For some reason I glanced up to the shelf behind the top of the back seat and saw my purse.

"Yes, it's in there, in my purse," I replied.

"Do you mind us having a look?" he checked.

"No."

"Where can we take the kids to?" he also asked.

There was only one person I knew who to call on. She was our dearest neighbour and I knew they'd be well looked after with her.

"To Mrs. Hawley's," I said, and told them where she lived.

"You're going to have to go to hospital to be checked over," the paramedic said when we were finished.

I hated hospitals and really didn't want to go, but I was given no choice. They didn't hold any chance of me surviving because the trauma of my head injuries was so severe – it was some "little accident"!

"Are you able to sit up?" he asked.

"Yeah," I replied. "But I don't know what's wrong with me!"

The paramedics carefully helped me out of the car and after I stood up, a tow truck pulled up. As I was walking to the back of the ambulance, with the paramedics holding me on either side, the truck's driver appeared beside us. I suddenly remembered something Clive had always said to me about crashing the car, so I turned to him.

"My husband said, if ever I was in an accident, I was to have the car taken home – not to a wrecking yard," I said. I gave him my home address, which thankfully was just down the road and around the corner. But it wasn't until I got to the front of the car that I saw just how much damage was done to it – the front was literally wrapped around the telegraph pole!

"Oh my God!" I cried. "My husband is going to kill me! I've ruined his car!"

"Don't worry about the car, Love," the paramedic said, ignoring my comment – all they were worried about was that I might have fainted on them, I suppose.

"Can you hop in the back?" they asked.

The step into the back of the ambulance was high, and I was only short. I nodded and started to climb in.

"Just lie down on the bed, Sweetheart," he said. "Don't worry about the car or the kids – the police will look after them."

The next thing I knew the ambulance was speeding on its way to the hospital. I don't recall hearing it's siren, and it's quite possible that I had passed out along the way there.

When they got me into the emergency hallway, I remember lying there for what seemed to be a couple of hours. It wouldn't have been that long, but to me, it was.

Clive had arrived there about an hour later by taxi. The police had phoned him and had told him to come to the hospital immediately, as they didn't expect me to pull through. In that few minutes he was allowed to be with me, I apologised to him for wrecking the car.

"Don't worry about the car," he said. "Just make sure you get better. I'll come back later and see you. I've got to go and check on the kids."

I learned later that he had seen my exposed brain, and he couldn't stay with me because it was too traumatic for him.

But there was some waiting as the doctor in the emergency department was debating on whether to start with me, or with a young boy who had been knocked off his bicycle and also needed immediate attention. The last thing I remember was the doctor saying to me, "I'm just going to put this needle in the wound to kill the pain."

I wasn't feeling any pain, but they gave me the needle, as they were about to stitch me up. *'Gee,'* I thought, *'for a little cut, they're going to an awful lot of trouble! I thought it only needed a band-aid!'* I don't remember anything after that because I must have blanked out.

Clive did return later with Hilda, at around nine o'clock. I was upset that he had brought her because I still didn't think that she needed to have gone out of her way. She lived nearly an hour away from us, so it would have been quite a drive for her to be here. I also didn't realise that he didn't have a car anymore and he needed a lift in!

They told me how Clive had rung both her and Mum to tell them what had happened, and then he had arranged for our wonderful Mrs. Hawley to look after the kids for him while he was with me. I was quite groggy, of course, and they left after about an hour, because, I thought, she had a long drive home. But in reality, they had to allow me to rest, and they were also worried that I wouldn't survive. They didn't know my determination to live…

I amazed the doctors in the hospital, for three times that night I had woken up from nearly dying. There were more doctors around my bed each time I opened my eyes, and whenever I dozed off, they would shake my arms, saying, "Wake up Mrs. Duncan! Are you okay?"

But I struggled really hard to stay with it.

"Please let me go to sleep, I'm tired!" was all I could say.

"No, we want you to stay awake, Mrs. Duncan," they insisted. Their reason for keeping me awake was in case I lost consciousness and died, so they tried hard to keep me awake and alive.

I survived that night enough to impress the staff the next morning, for they allowed me to try some breakfast cereal. I took some sips and got through it slowly, and it looked to them as if I had managed to eat it all without any problem.

But in fact, I had brought it all back up into the bowl, then covered it over with a napkin. Thankfully they weren't around at the time, because they would have made me stay there longer, and I was bright enough when the doctor came around later to check on me.

When he'd asked how I felt, and if I had any complaints with my head or the rest of my body, I promised him that I was fine. I *really* didn't like hospitals and I was determined to go home. I must have convinced him, as he allowed me to leave, providing I rested up and told my local doctor to check on me the following Monday; he had to check my stitches and make sure I was healing okay.

Clive was called to let him know I was being discharged and that he could come to collect me when he was ready. So he called a taxi and came in, and as soon as I was ready, we left for home.

Later that week he told me how grateful he was that I had pulled through, because on seeing how dreadful I had looked, and worse, seeing my brain, he thought I would've died that night. And the doctors had said to him to prepare for the worst, as they also didn't expect me to live through the night. He was scared he wouldn't see me sitting up the next day. But they didn't know my determination and I defied death for the sake of my family.

***

After I came home from the hospital, it was a slow recovery. On the following Monday, Clive rang our family doctor, Dr. Graham, for him to come and see me at home that day. When he arrived, he was shocked to see my head wrapped up in bandages.

"Oh my god! What happened to you?" he cried.

I told him what had led to my situation. He was surprised to see me sitting up in the recliner armchair.

"What the hell did they let you come home so early for?" he said, as he was taking the bandages off.

I tried to explain that I had felt fine when the hospital doctor had checked me the next morning, and that I must have seemed bright enough for him to let me go, (though I didn't mention how much I hated being in hospitals, or that I had brought up my breakfast).

"They should have kept you in there for another three or four days!" he insisted, then took a close look at my head. "Okay, I'm not going to do anything just yet," he began thoughtfully. "It's too early to take the stitches out."

He wrapped up my head again and gave me some pain killers – which luckily, at the time, I wasn't in a lot of pain.

"I'm going to come back and check in on you next week," he said, and left.

Two weeks after my accident on a follow-up visit, he closely examined the top of my forehead and had some interesting news.

"The stitches are starting to dissolve," he said, "so I won't have to worry about taking them out."

But I was now concerned about my hair, as it was starting to feel like rope and I wanted it washed, so I asked him about it.

"I wouldn't wash it if I were you at the moment," he said, "but you can soak your head in warm water. Not hot, not cold; in warm water. As warm as you can bear it."

So every morning before going to work, Clive would get me the big bowl that I had used to make the cake mixes in (which none were being made since the accident), and half-filled it with clean, warm water. He also found me a pool deckchair that was long and, when unfolded, sat fully flat and low to the floor.

He put a foot stool at the head end of the chair and sat the bowl on it, with a towel under my neck once I'd laid down. This way the bowl was both behind my head and just below it, and I was able to lay there for two or three hours each day, gently resting it in the water. He even placed the phone beside me so that I could answer it if it rang, and of course, Clive called me every day to see how I was going.

When my head started to get cold, and my neck or head felt sore, it was time to get up. That's when the sickly part came…

I got an awful shock when I saw the colour of the water, especially in the beginning. It was *red*! Bright red! I didn't realise at first that it was all the blood that had dried in my hair from the accident!

I'd wrap the towel around my head and take the bowl to the bathroom to empty it, and thankfully, with the daily soakings, the water got lighter and lighter. Often I would feel a bit dizzy, or weak, and so I'd go and sit in the armchair in the loungeroom until Clive came home in the afternoon.

The company he worked for was very kind to him. They had loaned him a dark green Morris mini-van until he was able to afford a new car, but as it became clear that it could be a long time waiting for this, they offered it to him at a very low price. He liked the mini and it gave him the transport he needed through the week, as well as allowing us trips to the shops for food or other important things, so he bought it.

There were only two seats in the front, with storage space directly behind them in the enclosed back cabin – enough room to fit four young children. Two small windows in the swing-out back doors let in some light, but the interior black paint and dark grey carpet made it a snug hiding place. We let the kids ride in there when we all had to go out somewhere together, and told them to duck down if we saw any police. Back then, cars may not have always had seat belts, but passengers were still supposed to be in seats.

Both Mum and Mrs. Hawley came over on regular intervals in the weeks that followed, checking in on me to see that I was okay and that the family was managing without me being able to do much for them. Mum came as often as she could, helping with looking after the children, or when Clive and I needed her. She had to get the bus because she couldn't drive, and Dad would have been using his car for work.

***

About a month on, when the water in the bowl was getting very clear, Dr. Graham said that I could start giving my hair a gentle wash. Clive came in very handy again, putting a bit of soap on my hair and softly running it through. Probably a month or two after that, the hair on the right side of my head started to fall out when I was brushing it! It didn't matter how carefully I stroked, more and more came out! I went partially bald there and it troubled me.

"Look at that! I'm going bald!" I said to him one day. It got so bad that I bought a cheap wig to hide this large patch. I was ashamed to be seen without it and I hated looking in the mirror, wondering if my hair would ever grow back normally again. It did come back, but it took a long time.

I went on getting stronger each day until I could start making and decorating cakes for the upcoming Easter show. I didn't want to miss out on entering the competition as it was fun, and it was like therapy for me, too.

As each day passed, I was on the road for good improvement, and it seemed all was going well for the future ahead.

As far as I know, I had gone on to make a complete recovery, however, within a year I would hear from my Dad in Spirit, and it was not too long when I could start to hear and see people in the spirit world…

৪০৫৪

Postscript

Although this book is about my life's journey up to about late 1973, it does not cover any of my spiritual experiences, as much of that came to me after my serious car accident. However, my premonitions were there from around age eleven. As a teenager, I was asked what I was going to be when I grew up? The answer was simple and I always said the same thing.

"A mother, and I'm going to have four kids; boy, girl, boy, girl."

"Why a boy first?" they would say.

"So the boy will look after the girl as they grow older."

It was something I just *knew*. And as it happened, I did have a boy, Arthur, a girl, Debbie, a son, Kevin, and a daughter, Christine.

When I was pregnant with Christine, I sensed my dad was always close to me. I saw his face on the side of a car that drove by one afternoon, and the car was the same model as the one he'd had, only it was a different colour. Clive saw him too!

I had foreseen car accidents, when babies would be born, or their gender, and also a tragic plane crash one week before it happened. The details of it were exactly true: the faulty engine in

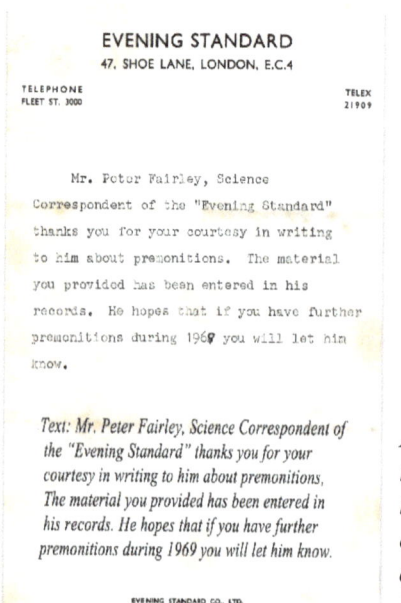

Text: *Mr. Peter Fairley, Science Correspondent of the "Evening Standard" thanks you for your courtesy in writing to him about premonitions. The material you provided has been entered in his records. He hopes that if you have further premonitions during 1969 you will let him know.*

A reply letter I received in regard to a magazine ad, asking people to send them their premonitions or spiritual experiences. I sent them my premonition of the plane crash (that appears in My Encounters of the Spirit World).

the left wing, the fire and the famous passenger jumping off the wing once it had landed.

But there was also the physical world and its ups and downs to deal with. Both of my daughters helped a friend of mine to start up a dance school, and they went on to perform at many venues. My sons were not as ambitious and enjoyed playing at home or riding their bikes.

When Arthur was about thirteen, he and Kevin decided to ride up to the big shopping centre of town late one afternoon. Helmets and other safety gear weren't mandatory to wear back then and it would cost them dearly. The direction they had taken to get there brought them to a wide, very busy main road, and they chose to cross it just near a slight bend. Sadly they were hit by a car, and both were badly injured. Unfortunately Arthur had received the brunt of it, and had actually died at the scene, but was miraculously revived after three minutes by the ambulance driver, who lived on that very corner and was just about to go to work!

In March 1984 we moved interstate. The kids were now in their teens and three of them were now working. On our long drive across country, just after we'd crossed the border into Western Australia, we received news that Clive's father had died. We had to hurry to get to Perth city so he could catch a plane back to Sydney for the funeral, while I stayed with the kids in a caravan park.

Around May 1984 we bought a house up in the hills of Perth, and on the very day we moved in, 9th June, my sister, Hilda, rang to tell us that her husband, Allan, had died. Allan was more than a brother by marriage; he and my husband had spent the greater part of their childhood and young adult lives together, going through school, even working in the same job at the same workplace. They were best friends as well as brothers-in-law.

Clive and I both went back to Sydney on the coach for the funeral, and afterwards, before returning to Western Australia, my husband and I went to visit his mother, not realising that this, too, was to be the last time we'd see her. Three days later we arrived back to our new home after a long and wearying coach drive.

Best mates: Allan (left) and Clive (right), Dundas 1958.

Within six months of leaving N.S.W. and only five months after Clive's father's death in April, we had a call from Brian, Clive's brother, telling us that their Mum, Ruby, had passed away. Brian bought us all tickets to get a coach back to Sydney for her funeral.

Clive's Mum and Dad in their back yard, shortly before we moved to W.A. (the shed we'd lived in with baby Arthur is just off to the right).

Employment in W.A. was also hard for us to get, and each of us changed jobs more than once.

It turned out to be tough trying to fit in with the people of the new area. There was a strong Christian following in the suburbs of the area and we were sort of 'expected' to go along to their church. The traumas of our recent family deaths were bad enough, but trying to be accepted in among these people was just as bad. It was the stuck-up people in the area we had to worry about the most.

We quickly found out that many West Australian's had a negative opinion towards anyone who came from the east (this may not still be the case). They seemed to like telling us, or 'reminding' us, that we were from "the eastern states" (not say, from Sydney, or Melbourne, Newcastle etc.).

We were told by numerous people that we had to be there three years before we would be accepted. This really upset us, as we'd never been treated so rudely before. After settling into our new home, we thought we would just ignore them and get on with our life and pretend they were just jealous.

But it seemed that because we were from "the eastern states", my family couldn't get real steady work, only casual and sometimes dirty work for the first twelve months. The saying that we had to be there for three years was painfully true. Clive couldn't find stable, long-term work anywhere. He was either too qualified or not qualified enough, but we knew it was because he was an "Eastern Stater".

From day one, we felt like aliens. We grew more and more distressed at how our move for a 'new beginning' was, on the whole, being not much more than an expensive undertaking. It was a very difficult time for us, and after about three years of trying to fit in, we decided to leave W.A. and return to N.S.W.

After the first year there, we agreed that in the following January, Clive would return to his old job in Sydney, while I would stay on in Perth with the kids and attempt to sell the house. For the next ten months we listed the house with several real estate agents but were unsuccessful in finding a buyer.

The distance and uncertainty of our time apart worked on us until it was almost excruciating. I could not give my husband any good news of a sale and the months seemed to drag on. We rang each other often and in one conversation, we talked about how little interest there was in people looking at the house. By about October 1985, he came back to live with us, very disappointed with the poor results of selling it.

We found out that the agents were turning prospective buyers away, which only added to our frustration. After listing the house with more than one agency, we met an English real estate agent around mid-April of 1987. He was new to the area and was looking for some business to get him started. We told him of our earlier dilemma with the local agents and he asked us to let him try selling it, promising us that, if we let him, "handle it his way", he would have it sold by the end of the month.

Reluctantly we agreed and in three weeks, he had scheduled an 'open house'. And guess what, an offer was made right in the first hour of inspection! Thirty minutes later we had a second offer that was slightly better than the first. We took it and within six weeks, we were packed and ready to move again. But Kevin, my youngest son, had fallen in love with a woman only months earlier, and Christine had a boyfriend by now, too. This made leaving W.A. much harder, as they missed their partners, and being teenagers, they were very moody about it.

By the first week of June we were off, our family was on our way back to N.S.W. We eventually found a house in Woy Woy, up on the Central Coast in what was, at the time, a nice, quiet area. By now our older daughter, Debbie, had moved to Queensland. It felt like our family was breaking up, as our kids weren't happy without their partners and tensions were high.

But we persevered. In January 1988, Kevin became engaged to his West Australian girlfriend and moved back there to live with her in her family's house where, in March 1989 they got married. Christine stayed on in NSW with her then boyfriend, eventually marrying him in 1990, but after several years, they spilt due to her husband's abusive personality. Debbie eventually moved back to our house on the Central Coast and became friendly with the man who lived next door. He was fine as a neighbour, but when Debbie became emotionally involved with him, he turned rather nasty.

But the final straw for us was in September 1997, on the weekend of Princess Diana's funeral. Saturday was Arthur's thirty-fifth birthday, and Debbie, Clive and I had shared a cuppa and a cake with him. He had been single all his life and had no children, either. He'd always wanted someone to love and when he finally met the girl of his dreams, she hurt him badly.

I understand now he had been suffering severe depression, anxiety, as well as schizophrenia. He'd also had to put up with dreadful bullying at work, especially from a few men who acted like bouncers for the girl that Arthur loved. The health system of the day simply didn't have the knowledge or resources for helping patients and families cope with loved ones in these conditions, nor did they seem to have the ability to provide successful treatment to patients. So we didn't know how to deal with his mood swings, strange behaviours or his deep loneliness.

That Sunday was also Father's Day. It was a sombre afternoon and evening with the way the world was affected by the princess' death. I thought Arthur's sadness was because of that, and when we said goodnight to him at around eleven o'clock, I tried to help him by saying that Princess Diana was in a better place now. He didn't give much of a reaction though.

The last words I had to him were, "Go and have a good night's sleep and we'll see you in the morning."

I then gave him a kiss on his cheek and a big hug and hoped he would be okay the next day. But it wasn't to be. I wasn't to know this was the last time I was to hug my son.

I won't go into a lot of detail here, as I have already covered this in both of my previous books, and it can be difficult for some people to read. In fact, if anyone is reading this who has lost a loved one or friend by a train accident, then you may want to know that the following could be a trigger for you (*please skip to ➡ on page 237*).

Our beloved son, Arthur at 30 y.o.

At around midnight I noticed that his bedroom light was on. Clive was sleeping beside me, but I couldn't settle out of concern for Arthur. I must have started to doze off around one-fifteen, but I woke when I heard the one-thirty-five a.m. train going north. We lived across the road from the main rail line between Sydney and Brisbane.

However, what I heard wasn't just the toot of the train' horn, (a sound that they make when approaching level crossings) – it soon became clear that the train driver was trying to warn someone of their approach.

That someone turned out to be my son.

The train's horn was blaring all the way down the line as it came closer to us, and its breaks were screeching as though they had locked up and were now sliding on the tracks. The sound of metal grinding on metal seemed to go on forever. I thought it would never stop.

Those eerie, awful sounds curdled my stomach, scaring me, just as they can do today – the memory leaves me feeling sick with fear.

Then came the thump – literally opposite our house.

Arthur's life had been one of incredible difficulty, and in an instant, it was gone. A big part of me went with him that night.

Clive was devastated, and has never been the same since. He was our beloved first-born child.

⇨ Our lives were turned upside-down with this experience and though we tried to continue living there, Clive's health took a battering and eventually we had to move. We found a lovely home up on the Mid North Coast where Christine was living, and we've been here ever since.

At fifty years of age, my hair where the car accident had split my forehead in 1974 started to go very soft, like a baby's hair, and it began to fall out again due to aging.

All these years later, Clive and I have celebrated our 62nd wedding anniversary on the 2nd of December 2023.

Me at 50 y.o.

***

My life has been a struggle, yes, but I've survived and I've been able to tell you my story. So I will leave this with you here and hope you enjoyed this journey with me.

And if you haven't already, then I also hope you will read my other two books, *My Encounters with the Spirit World* and, *Beautiful Spirits*, which are about my years encountering spirits and communicating their messages of love to the people they'd left behind. I'm sure that, if you like the subject of spirituality and the afterlife, you will enjoy and get comfort from them.

If you want to know more about me, please contact me via the links provided in the front of this book. I thank the people who have supported me in buying my other books, too.

*May I wish you good luck,
and may God bless you all.*

☙❧

The 'Boarding' House

FOOTNOTE:

Due to an editorial deadline with *Beautiful Spirits*, there was a missing paragraph to the story "The Boarding  House", which has bothered me, as it is important and also helps close that chapter. The following was meant to have been included with it.

When I was visiting my son and his family in Western Australia many years ago, I'd had this vivid dream that turned out to be connected – in real time – with a friend of mine in N.S.W.

In this dream, my friend, Julie, and I had gone on holiday somewhere, and we came across a boarding house. Because we were tired, we went in to see if we could rest up for the night. As we approached the front door, which was open, we saw people just standing around, looking glum. Some were sitting, but they seemed to be waiting for something. Although it didn't look very appealing, we thought it would be good enough to stay in for at least a night.

We walked in, looking for the owner or manager, and noticed a door open down in the nearby hallway. Someone went in there, and we thought this must be where the office was, so we waited in the foyer for our chance to see them too.

After a few minutes, the door opened again and another person was beckoned in. There were no words spoken, but somehow they knew it was their turn. Yet we never saw anyone come out.

The next time the door opened, Julie was beckoned in.

At last we can talk to someone, we thought.

But I was kept outside. Curious as to why, I waited, expecting to be seen very soon.

Several minutes went by and still nothing. I felt compelled to barge in there to see what was taking so long and made my way to the room, just in time to see her in a zombie-like fashion, bent like a backward banana shape, floating upwards to the ceiling.

I was deeply worried and ran to her, managing to grab her ankles and screaming, "Noo! Give her back to me! You can't have her!"

And then I woke up.

Though it was a dream, there was something that disturbed me with it, and it stayed with me for days.

The chapter ended there, but I have the opportunity to include the follow-up that was meant to be in it, here…

A week later – in real life – I arrived back home in N.S.W. I had wanted to talk to Julie about that dream, though I didn't want to worry her unnecessarily in case it frightened her. So I waited a few days until I had properly settled back into routine, and then phoned her to make a visit. The next day we caught up.

I was a little taken aback to see her rugged up in a blanket, sitting in a deck chair, soaking up the warm sunshine on her front veranda.

"Hi, is everything okay?" I asked her.

"Oh well," she began. "I've been in the wars a bit. But I'll get by."

I had been wondering if I should tell her about my dream, then on impulse, I did.

"I had a very vivid dream of you while I was away," I said, and went into the details of what I had seen. She was surprised and, when I was finished, she gave me an interesting response.

"My, that's strange," she said. "For, three days after you'd left, I was rushed to hospital with pneumonia. The doctors worked hard to help me breathe. Apparently I'd had a problem that they'd tried to fix, but I think I was close to death."

She'd flawed me with the news.

"I remember that I had heard you calling to me to come back! And I think I must have blanked out, for I don't remember anything after that until the next morning, when I woke up in a lather of sweat. I felt so hot, Joyce!"

I thought about the timing of her emergency to when I'd had my dream – it was about three days after I'd arrived at my son's house; the same day I had flown out from Sydney.

"The doctors were amazed that I pulled through the night!" Julie added, "because they thought they had lost me! Apparently they had stayed with me all night, monitoring me every five minutes."

We were both excited to piece our uncanny experiences together.

"They kept me in hospital for a few more days to make sure I was well enough to come home," she continued. "I only just got back three days ago, on the condition that I rest up! That's why I'm sitting out here in the sun! I didn't want to tell you in case you worried about me and cut your holiday short to get back to see me! But as you can see, I am doing okay! Thank you for bringing me back!"

I couldn't help but smile, so happy that I had made a difference to her dangerous health scare.

***

So I turn to you, the reader, and ask your thoughts on this story. Do you think that my dream and Julie's near-death experience really were connected? Do you think that perhaps they were only a coincidence?

Are you willing to believe in strange, unexplainable encounters with the spirit world?

I sincerely hope you have enjoyed my life's journey in this, and the other two books.

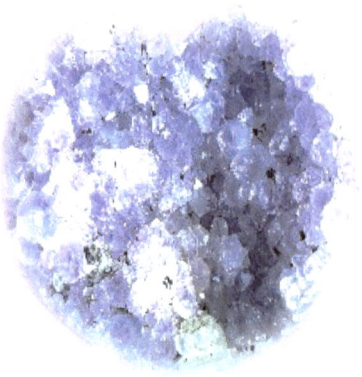

*My Amethyst Heart
- for Spiritual Love
and Guidance.*

Picture Credits i

Joyce at 12 months 3
Unknown Sunderland Photography Studio 1950

"Life in an air-raid shelter" 4
Source: Vintage Life, North London, England 1940

Firemen in London 5
This image is believed to be in the public domain; from the National Archives. *New Times Paris Bureau Collection (USIA)*

Modern Sunderland House 6
Clive.

Sunderland House back yard 7
David Duncan (Sr.) Ca. 1938

Stamped Ration Book 10
Source: Public domain getarchive.net

Child's Ration Book 10
Source: picryl media Internet-free source

Greenhouse on Allotment 12
Source: Pinterest

Dad near Allotment Ca. 1930/40's 13
Photographer: Unknown

A Larrikin Dad with mate Ca. 1930/40's 17
Photographer: Unknown

Young girl with pram 18
Source: Facebook group Australia Remember When; original source City of Sydney Archives, "Pittwater Online News" 1950. *Photographer: Unknown*

Sunderland under snow compilation 19
Sourced: Facebook group Sunderland History, *photo courtesy of Steven Edge-Robinson; photographer unknown*

English bus 26
Sourced: Facebook group Sunderland History, *photo courtesy of Steven Edge-Robinson Ca. 1960's; photographer unknown*

Dad beside farm tractor 27
Photographer: Unknown

Barnes Park Carving & Penshaw Monument 28
Christine K. Duncan

Picture Credits ii

Sunderland Map 29
Source: www.oldemaps.co.uk An old town map of Sunderland in Durham as shown on the Bartholomew Half-Inch map series of the mid twentieth century.

Family at Seaburn Beach 31
Photographer: Unknown Ca. 1948

English Canal 32
Clive

Dad's Mummy 41
Christine K. Duncan

Joyce, David & Hilda 42
Photographer: Unknown Ca. 1950

Grandma Hollywood 44
Christine K. Duncan; original photographer unknown

Scottish Railway Logo on Train 45
Clive

S. S. Cammeronia 46
Source: Facebook group Ten Pound Poms; *photo shared by Veronica Montgomerie*

Ship's Menu 49
Source: Facebook group Ten Pound Poms; *photo shared by Michelle Janes-O'Neil*

Rock of Gibraltar 50
Accession Nº: 1983.1191.36, *photographer unknown Ca. 1880-90's*

Crossing the Line 52
Source: Facebook group Ten Pound Poms; *photo shared by Veronica Montgomerie*

Sydney Opera House and Harbour 2023 57
Christine K. Duncan

Luna Park Circa 1950's 63
Source: Public Domain: Pinterest

Loco 5801 66
Public domain.

Picture Credits iii

Warragamba Town ... 67
Source: Facebook Group The History of Warragamba, photographer unknown

Warragamba House compilation ... 68
Christine K. Duncan Ca. 2009

Joyce with siblings & Nellie ... 70
Bernie Photography Studio 1951-2

Warragamba School Class ... 73
Source: Facebook group The Warragamba Public School OLD time yearly photos.

Joyce, 11 y.o. ... 77
Bernie Photography Studio 1951-2

Kids on slide ... 80
David Duncan (Snr.)

Wardrobe ... 82
Christine K. Duncan

David & Mate on stairs ... 83
Photographer: Unknown

Bedroom sketch & all floor plan sketches ... 84
Joyce B. Duncan; post effect Christine K. Duncan

Black Doll ... 85
Christine K. Duncan

Otford Station ... 87
Source: Heritage for NSW; Partial view of Otford railway station, south coast line NSW 1937, photographer unknown

Otford House ... 88
Hilda Janes 1955

Otford Village (aerial view) ... 90
Wollongong City Council photographer unknown Ca. 1948

Spelling Book ... 91
Christine K. Duncan

Angry bull (*illustration*) ... 93
A Lovers Quarrel by Randolph Caldecott Ca. 1890

Picture Credits iv

Vintage Telephone ... 94
Source: Facebook group Australia Remember When; *photo shared from Port Pirie History Photos Info and Random Stuff*

Joyce 15 y.o. ... 103
Clive 1955

Vintage Push Mower ... 105
Public domain

Clive & Mates ... 108
Allan Janes Ca. 1957

Epping Tennis Group ... 109
Clive Ca. 1956-7

Joyce, Taronga Zoo ... 110
Allan Janes

David Compilation ... 113
Christine K. Duncan; original photographers unknown

Warragamba Dam Power Station ... 116
Clive

Joyce's photo album compilation ... 117
Christine K. Duncan; originals Clive.

Joyce & 'Spot', Ettalong compilation ... 117
Christine K. Duncan; originals Clive.

Joyce 16 y.o. ... 120
Clive

Joyce in favourite dress ... 121
Clive

Joyce & Clive photo booth ... 123
Town Hall Railway Station, Sydney

Brenda & Joyce in Dundas kitchen ... 124
Clive

Clive at work ... 132
Clive Ca. 1959

John Sands games compilation ... 137
Christine K. Duncan

Picture Credits v

Engagement Ring 138
Christine K. Duncan

Family ball & Warragamba Dam invite 139
Allan Janes (Family Ball); Christine K. Duncan (Invite)

Mrs. Janes 144
Allan Janes

Hilda & bridesmaids 145
Photographer: Unknown

Clive & Joyce 21st Birthday 150
Allan Janes

Joyce and bridal party 153
'Hop-along" Tommy Macintyre

Dad's smile 159
Photographer: Unknown

Clive & Joyce wedding photos 162-3
'Hop-along" Tommy Macintyre

Joyce & Jean with babies 168
(Original) The Daily Telegraph, photographer unknown

Pyloric Stenosis diagram 173
Public domain; Pinterest

Gerry & Arthur 177
Clive

Arthur at house tap 178
Allan Janes

Our first home 180
Clive (rendered from a negative)

Baby Debbie 183
Clive

Debbie's Christening cake 185
Clive

Arthur & Susan Compilation 187
Christine K. Duncan; originals Clive or Allan Janes

Red Telephone booth 188
Christine K. Duncan

Picture Credits vi

Joyce, Arthur & Tess 193
Clive

Baby Kevin, front lawn 196
Clive (rendered from a negative)

Family dinner at club 200
Glamour Photos *photographer unknown 1961*

Kevin's first Christmas 202
Clive

Kevin 4 ½ y.o. 204
Peggy Lee Acting Agency, photographer unknown

Mum beside Dad's car 206
Photographer: Unknown

Dad Duncan 213
Allan Janes

Pink Maypole birthday cake 214
Clive

Joyce's cake orders book 214
Christine K. Duncan

Mouseketeers in Melbourne 218
Source: Facebook group Australia Remember When
Ca. 1959/60

Edelweiss_4 219
Source: *Wikimedia Commons, User:Ibex73*

Baby Karen at clothesline 219
Clive

Joyce's four kids 221
Peggy Lee Acting Agency, photographer unknown

Joyce's four kids with Santa 1972 222
Photographer: Unknown

Clive's Singer Gazelle 223
Clive (rendered from a negative)

Joyce & Dolphin 224
Coffs Harbour Dolphin Park, photographer unknown

Picture Credits vii

1963 Green Morris Mini Van 231
Public domain; Pinterest

Best mates Allan & Clive 235
Hilda Janes 1958

Ruby & Leonard 235
Kevin Bradney

Arthur on Quad bike 239
Christine K. Duncan

Edelweiss 240
Source: *Wikimedia Commons, Daniel Schwen*

Joyce 50 y.o. 240
Absolutely Gorgeous Studio Photography, Erina

Joyce 83 y.o. 241
Christine K. Duncan

About the Author

Joyce B. Duncan was born in 1940 in Sunderland, England. She emigrated with her family in January 1951 to Warragamba, N.S.W. Australia.

She had her first apparition in December 1951, aged 11. Since then she's had premonitions, and around the age of thirty, she learned to read plain deck cards with her Aunty May. This led to her attending the now closed, Parramatta Spiritual Church through the 1970's, where she learned to tune in to the Spirit World and hone her Gifts of seeing and hearing people who have passed over.

In 1984, her late son, Arthur, asked her to give these gifts away because, in his words, "it was evil". So, in being loyal to him, she did, but she had also asked Spirit to, "please come back if ever I needed you". She later found out that Arthur had been told by people of the local Christian churches that what she did was evil.

Then in 2006, after asking for her spirit friends to return, two grandmothers in spirit came to her, telling her to write a book about her spiritual experiences. This became *My Encounters with the Spirit World*. In 2012 she was told by one of those same spiritual ladies – Lydia – that she was to write a second book about the return of her spiritual gifts, which became *Beautiful Spirits*. In the course of writing these books, her spiritual abilities slowly returned, and gradually she could see and hear them again.

Later, in a wax art reading by her younger daughter, she was shown that she would have three books in all, and this one, *Memories From My Past*, completes the series.

It is her heartfelt wish to share her gifts and life experiences with everyone through these books, and she hopes her readers all enjoy, and draw comfort, from them.

> *"I now know we are all watched over by angels and spirit loved ones and they give us their love when we need it."*
> ~ Joyce B. Duncan

www.ingramcontent.com/pod-product-compliance
Lightning Source LLC
Chambersburg PA
CBHW042042290426
44109CB00001B/3